MW01116162

There is no one doing stu
making among teenagers li
deeply in God's Word; his s...........
and his grasp of today's youth culture is spot on. Roger not only has a mind
for disciple-making, but he has a genuine passion for it, as well — and
that's what sets him apart! By God's grace, Roger has been instrumental in
building and leading some of the most dynamic local church youth ministries
in the country. Having personally served under Roger's leadership both at
Trinity, San Antonio and First, Orlando, we have both experienced first-hand
the effects of the principles he writes about here. The ripple effects of his
investment in this all-important work are being felt across generations and
around the world. Whenever you want to excel at something, regardless of
what it might be, it makes sense to learn from the best. If a dynamic, God-
honoring, kingdom-impacting youth ministry is what you are after, then
start reading *Dynamic Discipleship* now!

Dennis and Kathy Blythe
Dennis: Executive Pastor, The Church at Brook Hills,
Birmingham, AL, former intern, FBC, Orlando, FL
Kathy: Teacher, Former Student Ministry Intern, First
Baptist Church, Orlando, FL and discipled by Roger
at Trinity Baptist Church, San Antonio, TX

Dynamic Discipleship reflects the message and ministry that has characterized
Roger Glidewell's life and work for decades. This convictional approach to
youth ministry is grounded in Scripture and the wisdom gained from years of
ministerial experience. Though the volume is brief, the content is powerful,
purposeful, and practical, with a focus on the mentoring and ministry skills
needed to prepare the next generation to take the gospel to the nations. I
am delighted to recommend this fine book, which contains insightful and
helpful applications for church leaders, parents, and students.

David S. Dockery
President, Southwestern Baptist Theological Seminary

I believe in the practice of disciple making. In fact, I believe it is the only
hope youth leaders have of transforming the world. In this book, *Dynamic
Discipleship*, Roger Glidewell does a thorough job breaking it all down and

helping his readers process how they can make this first-century art a regular part of their work with students.

Tim Elmore
Founder, GrowingLeaders.com

Having served as a student pastor and now a university professor who trains students for vocational Gospel youth ministry over the past 25 years, I was introduced early in my professional ministry life to Roger Glidewell and Global Youth Ministry. It was evident to me from that initial interaction and now continuous interaction over the last two decades that Roger Glidewell has a passion to see students come to know Jesus as Lord and Savior and become a full court follower of Christ. This is seen in *Dynamic Discipleship* as Roger lays out the foundation for youth pastors and youth leaders to keep the main thing, the main thing. *Dynamic Discipleship* is a great resource for anyone who has a passion to see students come to know Christ and then walk into spiritual maturity in their faith. Roger shares his insights into why discipleship is often not done and why people are often intimidated when thinking about it. He lays out a biblical case for what spiritual maturity looks like (Availability, Accountability, and Ability) and then gives some very practical steps in how youth pastors, youth leaders, and anyone who desires to make disciples can accomplish this.

Dr. Jonathan Geukgeuzian '99
Christian Leadership & Church Ministries Chair
John W. Rawlings School of Divinity
Liberty University

Church leaders, there are those God ordained leaders who are set aside by God to reach a generation and to lead the church in reaching their generation. Roger Glidewell is one of those leaders. His latest book, *Dynamic Discipleship*, is one that every church leader needs to have in their hearts and on their shelf. In particular, lead pastors need to know how to lead their church to reach and disciple this generation. I am so much better equipped to reach and disciple this generation because of Roger's labors in this book. If you long to reach a generation, this book is a must. Thank you Roger, for being God's man for the next generation.

Keith Joseph
Author, Pastor, First Baptist Church, Jackson, Ga.

I recommend *Dynamic Discipleship* to you! Roger discipled me to disciple others when I was fresh out of college, and God changed my life. God used Roger to help me to be a better husband, father, friend, and co-worker. This book shares Roger's wisdom and disciple making experiences through years of practice, and he continues to make disciples even now. Apply its biblical principles to your students and see how it will change them, as well!

Glenn Powell
Executive Pastor, Tallowood Baptist Church, Houston, TX.
Former petroleum executive, 30 years
Former Chief of Staff, U.S. Senate

Jesus invested a great deal into the teenagers that He called to follow Him, and they were developed in countless ways. Today there is that same great need to disciple young adults, and they need it from their ministry leaders—not from the world that they can so quickly turn to! In *Dynamic Discipleship*, Roger Glidewell gives a call to action to ministry leaders. He challenges them to view students as disciples who have potential to be developed in exponential ways. I am grateful for Roger, who has encountered and equipped countless teenagers in dynamic ways. Over the many decades of Roger's ministry, he has seen fruitful results through young adults becoming mobilizers of the Gospel of Jesus Christ. One of my greatest appreciations of *Dynamic Discipleship* is that there is a married connection between discipleship and evangelism. For any ministry leader who has the privilege of equipping and growing young adults, *Dynamic Discipleship* would benefit them greatly to disciple youth like Jesus did.

Kevin Rariden
Pastor and Director of Student Ministry
Evangelism Explosion, International

Dynamic Discipleship is a long overdue book. In my opinion discipleship in general and youth ministry discipleship specifically has been the most difficult challenge of the late twentieth and early twenty-first century church in America. And, in my thirty-three years of training youth leaders in more than thirty-three countries since 1975, I would submit that discipleship is also the most difficult challenge for international ministries as well! *Dynamic Discipleship* just may very well be the most powerful practical and effective work on youth ministry discipleship to date. All youth workers will do well to read it, study it, and apply it! Thanks, Roger, for this outstanding contribution to church youth ministry!

Dr. Randy Smith
Founder, Youth Ministry International (retired)
Founder/President of Great Commission Youth Ministry

I have known and loved Roger Glidewell for over 45 years. As a young teenage boy, God allowed me to be influenced and shaped by Roger's love for Jesus and students. In his latest work, *Dynamic Discipleship,* Roger continues to influence and guide me and others who love Jesus and students. His is a lifelong commitment to Jesus shared with us. Don't just read this resource but digest it. Allow God to encourage and equip you through one of His faithful servants as you read and learn from one who has devoted his life to serving God and others.

Paul Turner
Longtime friend and fan, WinShape College Program

Roger Glidewell's decades of youth ministry experience parallel my own. Both of us have spent our entire adult ministry years encouraging, speaking to, and training youth leaders in churches to do what Jesus did—and challenged all believers to do—"make disciples." I have watched Roger and walked along with him in his unrelenting pursuit of modeling disciple-making and equipping youth leaders to do the same. Yet all too often pursuing that vision has meant swimming against the tide of ecclesiastical structures with paradigms and programs that, instead of encouraging a relational disciple-making investment in teenagers, have mitigated against it. Nonetheless, Roger has never lost his vision. I hold an unparalleled admiration for Roger who, after decades of swimming successfully against that tide, continues to give the clarion call to "make disciples" of teenagers and personally invests in discipling relationships with the younger generation himself. Because of this I know of no one better qualified to write a book entitled *Dynamic Discipleship*. This new book of Roger's will instill in you the same vision that Roger has for "making disciples" like Jesus did!

Barry St. Clair
Founder of Reach Out Youth Solutions
Vice President of Global Youth Engagement with
East-West Ministries International

I highly recommend *Dynamic Discipleship* to anyone in ministry. Roger Glidewell is one of the most godly, gifted, and dynamic ministry leaders I know. God has used Roger to impact countless numbers of students, churches, and ministries around the world. Personally, I was blessed to grow up in Roger's youth ministry, so I know first-hand God's anointing on his life and his passion for growing disciples. Raising the next generation must be a priority for all of us in church leadership today. This book will help you do your calling better for God's glory. I'm so thankful Roger took the time to write down this God-given discipleship strategy. I am a product of Roger's ministry and the teaching you will find in this book. I encourage you to read this book and start applying it, so that your church, ministry, and the next generation will become dynamic disciples of Jesus.

Jeff Simmons
Senior Pastor
Rolling Hills Community Church, Nashville, TN

The centrality of Jesus' ministry was intentionally investing in those he called disciples, whom he later declared to be his friends. Many student pastors know this, but they are unsure of where to begin when it comes to discipleship. For many years, I have had the privilege to learn from and be discipled by Roger Glidewell. His pursuit of and relationship with Jesus are inspirational, and it has been one of my greatest joys to follow him as he runs, sometimes crazily, after Jesus. Through the years, I have witnessed Roger practice every biblical principle presented in this book, and I know from personal experience that it works. As we join God's mission by reaching every youth of all nations, may we do so "dynamically" and "explosively," following the example of Jesus, as Roger challenges us in *Dynamic Discipleship*!

Cameron Boothe
Roger's Beloved Disciple and Pastor of Students
Chet's Creek Church, Jacksonville, FL

DYNAMIC DISCIPLESHIP

The "Secret" to Explosive
Youth Ministry

ROGER GLIDEWELL

DYNAMIC DISCIPLESHIP: The "Secret" to Explosive Youth Ministry
Copyright 2023© by Roger Glidewell
Requests for information should be addressed to:
Roger Glidewell
9319 Highway 52
Chatsworth, GA 30705

Glidewell, Roger, 1949-
DYNAMIC DISCIPLESHIP: The "Secret" to Explosive Youth Ministry

Roger Glidewell is the founder and president of Global Youth Ministry and president of the Global Institute for Youth Leadership.

Printed in the United States of America

ISBN: 979-8-89316-099-4 - paperback
ISBN: 979-8-89316-100-7 - ebook
ISBN: 979-8-89316-325-4 - hardcover

TO MY GRANDSONS

Emmitt and Sawyer

My hope and continual prayer for you both is that you will make a lasting Kingdom impact. May you rise to His best and bless many. Passing along God's majesty and grace to the next generation, for me, is the goal—and gauge—of my own discipleship journey.

CONTENTS

FOREWORD

Discipleship is a conversation that fills church offices around the globe as well as countless book pages and conference topics as ministry leaders work to figure out the best recipe or the latest winning way. To get there, we need to begin with this important question: Do we even understand the core practice of developing and discipling youth? You are likely making disciples around you all the time in at least something. It may be your love of a certain team, the games you play, the movies you watch, or other things that are highly valued by you. I have four teenagers in my home, and I am constantly making them into disciples, but the daily question I must ask is what am I discipling them to be? And am I finding success at it?

For decades, Roger Glidewell has led students and influenced leaders at the local church level; the academic level, including developing and teaching youth ministry courses; the national level as a key youth ministry influencer to some of the largest churches throughout the United States; and the global level, sharing the hope of Christ with youth while developing and Equipping leaders.

In the 1980s, I was blessed to have Roger as my youth minister. His ministry transformed my life during a camp experience. By the time I met Roger, he already had numerous years of leading and growing a youth ministry as well as gathering other leaders from churches throughout the country to learn from each other how to disciple students to be followers of Christ. The ministry Roger was leading at the time had already grown to a significant size, seeing hundreds of students show up weekly with me being just one of them. However, even in the middle of numerous students, he understood that significance is not measured in the masses, but in the outcome of the individual. So many years ago, he began to focus his leadership and ministry development on truly discipling young people, looking to the example of Jesus and following as He commanded.

We all stand on the shoulders of someone, and I know one of the reasons I am in ministry today is because a leader like Roger cared enough to make sure a culture of discipleship was one that welcomed me where I was and grew me into who I was intended to be.

I am thrilled that you are holding this valuable resource in your hand, as you have taken an important step to allow yourself to be coached well by someone who has worked through the dynamics of discipleship. In *Dynamic Discipleship*, Roger will help you identify potential disciples and discipleship candidates, and then help you to develop the youth in your ministry to become future disciple makers. This book is a deep well of wisdom and will put plenty of tools in your toolbox as you lead your youth to not just be a consumer of the Gospel, but a conduit.

J. Roger Davis
President, YM360

ACKNOWLEDGEMENTS

I could write a book just about the people who cared for me, worked with me, assisted me, supported me, guided me, and, yes, discipled me, all through my life's journey! It's so humbling to know that even in those times when I have been discouraged with myself, filled with awareness of all my shortcomings, still there were people who stuck by my side.

Most amazing among them is my wife, Kathi, who opened our home regularly for decades to all manner of young disciples. As a fellow discipler, she went beyond the call: she fed them, listened to them, taught them and counseled them…sometimes into the wee hours. My sons, Matthew and Justin, were present for discipleship from their infancy, being bounced on the knee of this or that teenager, oblivious to the conversations until they became teenagers themselves.

And then there were those adults who discipled me. Brother Gary Taylor, my pastor as a teenager, discipled me before I even knew it was a thing. I am forever indebted to him and probably would not have written this book were it not for his patient efforts on my behalf. Others followed during my college years to take up the arduous task of helping me stay on track, like Charlie Nobles, Larry Maddox, David "Squeak" Martin, and my college dean, Bill Rogers.

I am especially grateful for the Rock House guys at Trinity Church. It was there with those amazing college-aged interns that I began to seriously invest in discipling future disciple makers. Jay Daniel, Philip Fields, Jim Graham, Cliff Heck, Glenn Powell, Rob Wood, and so many others graciously allowed me to invest in their lives. They in turn invested in our older high school students. The results were phenomenal, the stuff of stories we retell to anyone who will listen to this day.

And there were many amazing adult volunteers who supported the discipling effort at every church! At First Baptist Church, Orlando, many adults discipled hundreds of students and interns. As I write, it is my privilege to disciple a former intern's son at the Global Institute!

In the past two decades at the Global Institute, we have grown and developed and adjusted our discipling effort as we learned from both successes and failures. Hundreds of young men and women who were discipled here went on to become pastors, missionaries, deacons, worship leaders, corporate executives, and yes, disciplers! I cannot begin to name all of them. Truly, they were *my* teachers as I worked to gain a deeper understanding of what discipleship really looks like. A special thanks to the interns who worked through this manuscript with me: Emma Bookout, Daniel Johns, Emily Watkins, and Laura Whitaker.

I owe so much to so many. I have learned through good experiences and bad, from successful discipling experiences, and from failures. Even the flawed experiences where I messed up were helpful teachers to make me even more determined to get discipleship right. I'm still learning.

Thank you, one and all, from the bottom of my heart. You helped write this book. I pray that I have faithfully represented our discipleship experience; it has been a most rewarding and fulfilling part of my personal ministry journey. Only heaven will truly reveal how so many of you went on to contribute and multiply the effort with others who followed in your footsteps. We joyfully await that great day in Heaven when all of this will be fully realized.

PART ONE

SECRET TO OUR SUCCESS

Discipleship Dynamics

CHAPTER 1

WHAT IF YOUR YOUTH MINISTRY COULD SOAR?

Building on a Biblical Base

What if the youth in your church's youth ministry could experience Jesus' presence the way those first century believers did? What if your youth group could overcome great odds to become a powerhouse for Jesus? Would you go for it? Would you attempt the seemingly unattainable?

Your youth can. Jesus Himself is waiting for you to believe. This biblical reality has occurred before in young lives across the centuries and even to the present day. And it can happen again if you are willing. With your own young people! The first and greatest challenge is not whether your teens are willing to follow. The first and greatest challenge is whether you will believe, now, before your young people believe and catch His vision for them and for their world.

You must believe in God's best for your students. If you do, then truly all things are possible. Consider: if you are the youth leader, then you are like their Moses. You are the one who should paint

23

a picture of their God-sized future. But what is that picture? Fair question. Maybe we should begin by asking, "What will God honor?" If we want to devote ourselves to serve Jesus among young people, then what exactly does God want? What is His picture of fruitful youth ministry? What else, in the end, will matter?

RECOGNIZE THE SPIRITUAL GROWTH STAGES

If we are going somewhere, we want to know the destination, and then determine how to get there. Our amazing discipleship destination is Jesus. We want to look like Him, live like Him, and faithfully lead others to love Him as we do.

How do we get there? You have probably already encountered the biblical concept of spiritual growth in your faith journey. The sanctifying process—part of God's plan for our spiritual growth— was identified by the Apostle John in 1 John 2:12–14. There he outlined three stages of our journey toward spiritual maturity:

- Spiritual Child (Availability Stage) *"I am writing to you, little children…"*
- Spiritual Youth (Accountability Stage) *"I am writing to you, young men…"*
- Spiritual Father (Ability Stage) *"I am writing to you, fathers…"*

John was writing to believers at all stages of growth in the faith family, regardless of biological age, to identify how we grow into the likeness of Christ. The concept of spiritual growth stages was covered in detail in my previous book, *Youth Ministry by The Book.* Then, in *ReGroup* we explored the first formative stage of youth ministry, the Availability stage. In that book we looked at the practical steps involved in laying a good foundation for spiritual growth in young believers in your group. This book will pick up from there to explore the next stage, Accountability, in more detail. The goal is to prepare students for the final stage, Ability, which is the leadership stage.

Before we dive into discipleship (Accountability), let's determine what stages are currently represented in your group and how these stages shape the overall personality of your youth group. Every youth ministry is unique, and much of this is due to the mix of spiritual growth levels. It's not that hard to discern the levels represented in your group. So, let's do some evaluating together.

The Apathy Zone—Parked on the Launch Pad?

First, we should probably acknowledge the reality that you may have group members in your youth ministry who don't even qualify for the Apostle John's list of three stages of growth. After all, his letter only addressed believers. Although this additional group is not represented in the three stages mentioned by the Apostle John in 1 John, they are almost certainly in your youth group. And this is a good thing.

A good thing, that is, if they are being drawn toward life in Jesus and are not collectively hindering the group's spiritual growth.

Where should we place the youth who attend your activities but not because of any discernible spiritual interest? They participate, but they are not believers, though some may think they are, based on externals. We would like to think of these teens as at least pre-Christian. Still, right now this group is spiritually unengaged. We call this stage spiritual "Apathy" for that reason.

This group might represent a higher percentage of participants in some youth groups than any of us would prefer to think. But honestly, if they weren't in your youth group, where else might they be and what else might they be doing?

How would students behave who are in your group but not spiritually active believers? That would be Apathy level students who are in the youth group, but not really in Christ . . . yet. What excites them? If your group dwells mostly in the spiritual Apathy zone, you will know it. Why? Because your youth group will tend to be characterized by some measure of spiritual indifference. You will often observe these telltale traits:

Spiritual radio silence

There may be a lot of activity and good times coming from this group. But for these young people the good times won't be centered in Jesus. You are more likely to hear about the latest movies, song hits, and sports stats, along with your culture's normal coarse joking, put-downs, and worldly priorities. But Jesus? Radio silence. If Jesus does spill out, it will likely be in passing, or when prompted by an adult . . . or even as a curse word, but not in prayer. Or praise. And speaking of praise, don't expect these teens to open their mouths to enthusiastically sing the praises of Someone Else in worship. Their focus is on drawing attention to "me."

We don't get down on them for this. After all, unbelievers by their very nature do not worship God, much less praise Him for all that He has done to provide for them or protect them. That wouldn't be natural for them.

Social focus

Basically, spiritually Apathetic youth in your group will be all about the social interaction available to them in the youth group. Who's who in the zoo? Competition and conflict will often characterize these youth.

All the normal assortment of suspects may be present in this group: boyfriend/girlfriend items, the ninth-grade girl clique and accompanying outcasts, those loud-mouth guys whose every word is designed to impress the girls (mostly without success), and so on.

Self-centeredness

Among these youth, Jesus will probably get only lip service while they generally focus on putting themselves—not Jesus—at the center of attention. It's all about getting, not giving. The fruit of the Spirit will probably not be discernable. After all, the Spirit does not yet dwell in them. They will rely upon themselves and those around them for all their needs. And their drive to meet personal needs will be abundantly evident. They will tend to see others mostly as a means to meet their own needs.

The Availability Stage—Shake, Rattle, but no Roll?

The Apostle John explained that "spiritual children" (Availability) had been forgiven of their sin and have a joyful relationship with their loving Father. As newborns, they are enthusiastic about life in Christ and eager to please God. Although they don't know much, they do have assurance of their salvation.

How would students behave if the group consisted predominantly of spiritual children? These are youth who have come to faith in Christ but who are very childlike in their walk with Him. At this level, you will see spiritual enthusiasm. Chaotic, perhaps, but life in Christ will be discernible as these students may be:

27

Noisy

Spiritual children know they are loved. My toddler Justin would often come with his mom to visit my office at the church office suite. Upon arriving, Justin would run to every office on the hall announcing, "I'm here!" He received a joyful reception, along with candy and kisses. He knew he was loved! God's spiritual children know they are loved by their heavenly Father.

If there is any spiritual life at all in the group, you will hear plenty of joyful noise. Babies are noisy and full of life. Granted, the noise may not always be the noise of awesome praise and worship. Or the noise of the students all asking questions at once about God's Word, unless it's, "Hey, Johnny hid my Bible, and he won't tell me where it is!" Or "Are we finished with the lesson yet?" You may even hear sounds of whining if your activities are not active enough.

The noise levels will signify joy in the Lord. But be discerning: it may be a mix with Apathy noises. Why? Because in many youth groups spiritual children have been pampered too long, protected too much, and spoon-fed too many sweet devotional snacks instead of spiritual meat from the Word. The noise will become loud noise, as in horsing around noise, or fussing noise, or well, "feed me" noise. But because some youth programs have not done a very thorough job of preparing spiritual children for spiritual young adulthood, it may not be easy to distinguish this group from the Apathy group. It's one thing to be a legit spiritual child. It's another thing to stay childish forever.

Needy

Clearly, the babies will make it known they need to be fed! They may know how to put the bottle to their mouth, but someone else must prepare and then feed them the bottle. The childhood level of spiritual maturity has its special challenges. A group with mostly spiritual children can turn you into a traffic cop, school guidance counselor, and wet nurse all in one. You may hear a lot of "baby talk" from this group. Unless . . .

Unless you have begun to wean them from spiritual milk by beefing up their menu over time. Serving milk for too long can stunt growth. If they taste solid food, their desire for Scripture will increase. But their attention span will be shorter. And comprehension? Well, you should expect to repeat your teaching points often.

Non-welcoming

Have you noticed how children mark their territory? "That's my toy!" "No, I had it first!" Spiritual children may seem insensitive to others' needs and jealous of the attention of their parents. Small children sometimes cling to their parents in the presence of strangers. So it is in the spiritual realm, as well. If your group is characterized by this baby stage of spiritual maturity, this could mean that they will not be very welcoming to newcomers. Especially if they have been overly pampered, they may have difficulty welcoming or including others. In some youth groups, this reaction only manifests itself on the rare occasion that there actually *are* newcomers. I've seen this happen quite a few times: a new teen attends the group and will sit by himself on the edge of the group. The teens may or may not even acknowledge his presence. Some group members don't welcome him, talk to him, or sit beside him.

Clearly, if the youth group has a lot of spiritual children who are not growing, their focus may be on whatever is *for* them. They may be demanding for attention; but it is likely to be more focused on getting attention from the leaders than only from other teens, as with Apathy level teens. They have not yet considered that ministry is better when it is *by* them and for others.

REPOSITION YOUR GROUP FOR WHAT'S NEXT (ACCOUNTABILITY)

As everybody has a unique personality, so does your youth group, often based upon the mix of spiritual growth stages. These first two levels of spiritual growth, Apathy and Availability, comprise the largest percentage of participants in many youth groups. Such groups often seem distracted and unfocused. That's because they *are* usually just that! This is not an altogether bad thing. The children are doing what children do, and we love them. But we don't want them to stay that way, either spiritually apathetic or childish and needy.

Or do we?

Some youth ministries display acquiescence to this kind of spiritually childish behavior as though it is normal (and perhaps even should be this way?), and their group personality will reflect that maturity level.

What then do you have? Such a youth ministry is little more than a spiritual nursery. Perhaps we think that by keeping them happy and entertained, we can keep them coming to church . . . into their adult years.

Nope. Trust me, most of them will find other ways to be entertained later. Worldly entertainment is plentiful, affordable, and easily accessible. And let's be honest, often more attractive, as well!

Start With—But Don't Stay At—
These Two Lowest Growth Stages!

Many spiritual children come into the youth group as baby believers. But they may also exit the youth group the same way they entered. They either move on, remaining as spiritual children in adult bodies, or they just move on from—and out of—the Church.

You don't have to settle for this. In fact, if you make room for the next stage of spiritual growth, Accountability, you may begin to experience more rapid and steady growth even among the younger levels. The younger students will see real spiritual growth in the older discipleship students, and they will want to match it, even surpass it.

And that next stage is the too easily overlooked but incredibly essential secret of youth ministry. Accountability, the bridge between spiritual childhood and mature adulthood, should be the primary focus of youth ministry. That exciting stage is the subject of this book.

What if at least a few students in your youth group are ready for the next spiritual stage of maturity? Then you may be on the verge of some great days ahead. Perhaps you are beginning to see a healthy spiritual family emerge in which several stages of spiritual maturity are identifiable in your group. Some are ready to move beyond Availability (spiritual child stage) to embrace the "young man" stage described by the Apostle John in 1 John 2:12–14. He outlines three unique qualities of this next stage of spiritual growth. Let's take some time to identify the growth components of Accountability.

Character (Heart): They are Strong

The Apostle John says spiritual "youths" are strong, which means not weak! While some teens become preoccupied with their outward appearance, these teens are growing where it really counts; they know that "*bodily exercise profits a little, but godliness is profitable for all things*" (1 Timothy 4:4). They seek the stamina to stand against the influence of the Devil and the carnal fleshly nature. They do not easily succumb to the ungodly influence of the world, the flesh, and the Devil. They do not behave one way in one crowd but a different way in another.

These spiritually growing students have demonstrated that they are learning to stand on the authority of God's Word. They are not easily distracted or influenced by ungodly temptations. They are becoming a danger to the Devil. As Paul urged in Ephesians 6:10, they desire to "*be strong in the Lord and in the power of His might.*"

Confidence (Head): The Word of God Abides in Them

Some church teens are more likely to reflect worldly values than biblical principles. But these youth are searching for a more authentic and intentional walk with Jesus. The Apostle John says spiritually strong youths desire to have the Word *in* them, not just *on* them. They are reading the Bible on their own. They want to study rather than "skim" the Bible to gain a deeper understanding of Truth. They are beginning to memorize verses on their own. Yes, memorize: "*Thy word have I hid in my heart that I might not sin against you*" (Psalm 119:11 NKJV). And they meditate on Truth hidden in their hearts throughout the day. More impressively, they desire not only to read Scripture, but also to responsibly apply it to their lives as they learn from it.

Competency (Hand): They are Overcoming The Evil One

And what does applying Biblical truth look like? The Apostle John says they are *"overcoming the evil one."* They are on the battlefield, not hiding in the church "barracks." They are using the *"sword of the Spirt, which is the word of God"* (Ephesians 6:17) to resist evil and cause the Devil to take flight. They are whipping his tail.

You don't have to look long to identify these youth. First, they are becoming Equipped with a relationship with God. Second, you can see their battle scars from taking some hits; they have been wounded in their spiritual battles (Evangelizing). But they also have war stories to share with their fellow teens about their victories! And last, they are energizing other believers (Encouraging). We will discuss these qualities in more detail later. These warriors are becoming overcomers, and their success is impacting both their lost acquaintances and fellow believers.

Do you observe students in your youth group who are at least moving in this direction? They are like gold to your group. They may be clay-covered with jagged edges of rock, but the glitter of gold is beginning to shine through. Discovering and refining them is the discipleship objective.

REASSESS YOUR STUDENTS' READINESS FOR BLAST OFF!

How do you know that you have students in your group who can help lift the rest of your group to the next level? You can tell in several ways; some are positive while others may seem negative. But both indicate a plea for more challenges, not less, from these students!

Some Positive Indicators

Teens who may be ready for discipleship are often involved and eager to attempt greater things in their spiritual life. They are ready for discipleship when they ask or say:

- "I've been thinking about getting a new Bible; what is the deal with different versions?" Ding, Ding! Possible Discipleship Candidate (DC)!
- "What was that verse you mentioned in the Old Testament? I couldn't find it." Ding, Ding! DC!
- "I have been trying to share Christ with my friend at school who says she is an atheist. Do you have some verses or something for me to read that will help me with her?" Ding, Ding! DC!
- "Is there anything I could do around the church after school? I want to help." Ding, Ding. DC!
- "Do you think we could have another time besides Wednesday night for a special Bible study?" Ding, Ding. This may be several DCs!

These are some of the exciting signs that a young believer is ready for the next step, moving from follower of Jesus to disciple of Jesus. These are indicators that a youth pastor prays for! And that next step is the subject of this book. But be sure of this: if you don't feed this hunger, it may well diminish or lead the student to seek spiritual growth elsewhere.

A Not-So-Positive Indicator

I will let you in on a little surprise: some students who are ready for discipleship may be your complainers!

Hang on. Here's the deal: suppose your older teens come to you upset at the juvenile games being played during youth meetings. You want to help, but what will you do to placate these whiners?

- Change the midweek youth program to eliminate all games?
- Add another Bible study just for high schoolers?
- Offer additional service projects for older students?
- Ignore the complainers?
- Encourage those students to do their own Bible study?
- Split your group into high-school and middle-school groups?

Some of these responses may seem to have merit. The last one is a frequent go-to solution for many youth leaders. Perhaps they think it is time to separate the older from the younger on a permanent basis. This may seem like a good idea, but don't take this step lightly. Take time to prayerfully evaluate the long-term effects of splitting your teens into permanent older and younger groups. Why, you ask?

First, realize that this could potentially double your programs and workload. And another potential downside of a permanent separation is that your older teens often lose the opportunity to serve as positive role models to the younger students. To avoid these pitfalls, you might separate your older and younger teens for some things (small groups?), but not for everything.

What if some of your high school students are really only trying to tell you that they are hoping for accelerated growth? It comes across as a criticism, maybe even an insult to your leadership. But it may not be about that at all. At any rate, merely separating permanently into age groups does not necessarily solve the *spiritual* age problem!

Small groups may address physiological developmental stages, but discipleship should address their spiritual growth stage.

These students' complaints could indicate that they realize that following Jesus involves more than what they have experienced thus far (a good thing, right?). They are trying to find a way to express their desire to grow, albeit in a rather negative and juvenile manner. Shocker.

What if their discontent could become the gateway to discipleship?! The answer might be to spend more time working with students who are ready for a spiritual (not physiological) age boost. You don't need to separate every older student in the youth group forever from the younger students to accomplish that. Instead, a discipleship option could offer a step-up opportunity for the older students who are really ready to move forward in their spiritual growth.

You could be on the cusp of some exciting days ahead by making strategic decisions now! It may be time to fuel up for a launch into the next stage!

REDIRECT SOME STUDENTS TO CROSS THE BRIDGE INTO ABILITY

You will want to move these young people through Accountability and then on to the final stage of servant leadership in your group. The "father" (Ability) is identified as one who one has "*known him who is from the beginning*" (1 John 2:14). He has endured in the Faith, thriving even in persecution. This believer has earned the right to lead by bringing others to Christ and then by serving as a godly role model for those new believers. Your young people willingly follow these teenage believers into battle because they have observed their endurance through thick and thin.

The Ability stage is definitely possible in youth ministry. This level is not just about physical maturity; it is about spiritual maturity. Believe me, you want this stage represented in your youth ministry.

This book is devoted to the enthusiastic pursuit of the middle stage of spiritual maturity through discipleship among young people. Why? It is the steppingstone, the bridge, to student leadership (Ability). Why should anyone bother with discipleship? Why should we take on the difficult task of holding teenagers responsible for growing spiritually? Simple. Spiritual maturity in Christ is a worthy—even vital—objective. Discipleship is the biblical pathway to grow believers into mature leaders. As we obey this biblical mandate, we will see spiritual leaders emerge in the youth group, yes even in their high school years. The Apostle John calls them spiritual "fathers" for a good reason. These youths have earned the right to lead younger students in the group. And *that* will be worth all the sacrifices you will have made.

Just wait for young people to rise up and lead your group to reach their world for Jesus! You (and they) will be forever grateful that you made the effort to cross that bridge of spiritual Accountability into a far more fruitful and exciting youth group that lies just ahead!

It took me several failed attempts to realize that I had to provide growth opportunities at incremental levels of students' spiritual interest:

- Small group Bible study (Sunday school, in many churches) is about application of Scripture to life. It should make students hungry for more of the Word. It is like a nest for baby birds. The goal is to nurture them to keep growing stronger. (More on this in my book *ReGroup*.)

- Discipleship is the next step beyond small groups. It is far more than feeding milk to babies; it is more about holding learners Accountable for feeding themselves. The goal is to coax them out of the nest. The mother bird must not continue to feed them forever. Students must be hungry enough to want to feed themselves. Discipleship involves showing birds where to hunt for food, so they are not dependent. Good parenting, as any momma bird will demonstrate, involves teaching the hatchlings to hunt. This middle stage is the subject of this book.

- Mentoring is the final stage in the process. This Ability relationship is more of a one-on-one undertaking in which a mature leader guides a would-be leader to take flight into leadership in a side-by-side journey. (Shameless plug: this is the subject of my next book on the Ability stage.)

Discipleship is the bridge that we desperately need to build for students to cross from childhood into mature faith . . . as soon as possible.

One Tiny Caveat

The title of this book is not meant to imply that you can light a match and boom! Your ministry explodes. Sorry, no "instant assembly line" discipleship here.

No, this dynamite has a long fuse. The process of discipling students takes months and years before you can see the fruit of it. Yes, you read that right: I believe it may take a couple of years to realize the kind of growth explosion that will honor God and multiply His Kingdom. But it will also be the source of amazing stories to tell for decades after your young people have graduated. They will tell their own children these stories when they become teenagers!

But trust me, your efforts to disciple students will pay dividends here on earth, and more importantly, in Heaven. Which is where you want it to count anyway, right?!

Now, let's get ready to soar!

CHAPTER 2

IS DISCIPLESHIP REALLY THE SECRET?

Moving toward Dynamic Youth Ministry

Well? The chapter title poses a great question: Is discipleship really a secret? Is it even a big deal for youth ministry? Short answer: discipleship is not just a big deal; it is the most significant function of youth ministry in the local church! According to Ephesians 4:11-13, a youth leader's foremost task is to Equip the saints for mature ministry. Discipleship is the secret to strategic and dynamic youth ministry, the pathway out of superficiality. And that seems to be a secret that is held back from—and holding back—many youth groups.

We know that godly parents are ideal as disciplers. But many teens are coming to us whose families are uninvolved with church life. If you are a youth leader, you are the one your church depends upon to organize and guide discipling efforts with your young people. This should not be a secret to you. Rather, it should take center stage in your ministry with teens. Let's examine why discipleship should NOT be a secret to you or to your young people.

IT'S NO SECRET . . . THAT JESUS EXPECTS US TO DISCIPLE

Before Jesus ascended to Heaven, He left the disciples with one mandate: "*Therefore go and make disciples.*" You knew that verse, the Great Commission in Matthew 28:18–20. It is not a suggestion. It is the Biblical means by which we reach the whole world! The goal is not to make church attenders. The goal is to make disciples who become disciple makers!

Why, then, does disciple-making seem so obscure to many teenagers?

1 John 2:12–14 identifies children, youths, and fathers. Discipleship constitutes the second stage of spiritual growth that goes beyond childlike Availability to Jesus. This Accountability stage forms the bridge between spiritual childhood (Availability stage), and maturity in Christ (Ability stage). This was the bridge that Jesus led His disciples to cross to become overcomers.

Overcomers?! Now, that's a goal worth pursuing! This seemingly "obscure" or even "secret" growth stage separates great youth ministries from spiritually superficial groups. You cannot hope to develop spiritually healthy individuals—or groups—if they never exercise. And good luck if their spiritual diet consists of spiritual milk, or worse, sweet Bible snacks!

Casual intake is not enough. We must move our youth beyond mere Bible knowledge to acquire an appetite for seeking—and applying—Truth. We can't neglect students' spiritual exercise and still hope that they will develop the spiritual muscle they need to live effectively outside the comfy "nest" of their home and church family. Students in such a youth group may well be destined to become spiritual weaklings and losers, both now and (probably) for the rest of their lives, unless and until someone challenges them to exercise and train to become overcomers.

The lack of Accountability for one's self-discipline—which is the defining feature of discipleship—is a great weakness in the Church, not just in youth ministry. But this level is particularly crucial in youth ministry because our job is to wean students from being spiritual babies who must always be taken care of to become spiritual youths who, at the very least, have learned to take care of themselves. Discipling young people would not be a secret to Jesus.

IT'S NO SECRET . . . THAT LIFE DEMANDS GROWTH

Think about it: what should be the end goal for the twelve-year-olds who arrive at the door of the youth group room each year? Surely there is an objective, right? After all, we do not expect parents to feed their children forever, but to teach them how to feed themselves. Life demands that children grow up to be independent. Shouldn't we expect some measure of growth in their spiritual maturity after six or more years in youth ministry?

At some point, most parents shift their focus from what their children should learn to how they will learn for themselves. Similarly, youth ministry should serve this purpose in teens' spiritual growth. Sadly, too many church teens are living off their elders' faith. Young believers should take responsibility for their own growth. But many do not. In his book, *Youth Education*, Bill Benson says youth years are the ideal time to teach methods and tools of Bible study.[1] In other words, this is the time when they must learn to feed themselves.

My own church teaches the priesthood of the believer, but we somehow seem to overlook or even ignore the incredible responsibility involved in that. Many students and adults have never been weaned from spiritual spoon-feeding. If they are fed at all, someone else must feed them.

When my sons were small, I loved to sit them in the highchair and feed them . . . so long as I held the spoon. But when I relinquished the spoon to them, terror broke out in the kitchen! My son Matt would gleefully feed the entire room. It seemed to take him forever to learn where his mouth was! Gradually, he fed only the floor, his highchair, and his hair, often ending up wearing his cereal bowl on his head like a helmet!

Spiritually speaking, too many youth groups are wearing bowls on their heads. They don't know what to do with either the bowl or their eating utensils. The question is, when do we relinquish the spoon? We must help teens learn to hold the spoon, to grasp the bowl. That is the only way they will learn how to feed themselves! Eventually, they will find their mouths. Do we expect our youths to personally study the Bible or have daily quiet times? If we don't, they become sitting ducks for Satan, doctrinal dummies who are sent into life's battle with no ammunition.

It is often easier just to tell young people what the rules are rather than to explain to them the biblical principles behind those rules. They are told how to behave and what to believe, but never told why these things matter in the real world.

"Yours is not to question why,
Yours is but to do or die."
—*Author Unknown*

Taking shortcuts like that is a risk that we cannot afford. At some point, your teens must understand the reasons behind all those rules for living. We must walk with them through the study of the underlying principles found in the Scriptures so they can learn for themselves why the rules exist. And since discipleship is the great bridge to mature adulthood, shouldn't it be an incredibly significant concern for youth ministry? Children's ministry passes young people to youth ministry that then passes them on to adult ministries in the church. In my view, the ultimate test of effective youth ministry is whether it has enabled spiritual children to move through the spiritual youth stage into full maturity as spiritual adults, prepared to meet the challenges of life in Christ. Isn't it fair to ask how well we are doing this as youth leaders?

Accountability involves holding others responsible for learning how to take care of their own lives. That level is an essential part of growing up, learning how to behave as a self-disciplined individual. Parents, youth leaders, and the Church should view Accountability as the next essential step in spiritual growth beyond spiritual childhood.

Of course, we would not advocate that students skip their childhood. Likewise, we do not begrudge new believers their spiritual childhood. However, neither should we indulge them to remain forever as children. If we do, we should not be surprised when so many of them stray from their spiritual roots later in life. It is then that students begin to realize that their underdeveloped faith is inadequate to stand the test of everyday life in the real world. They recognize too late that they do not have adequate answers to those who dismiss or mock the Faith. Nor do they know how to find answers from Scripture when they face future crises, and neither parents nor youth leaders are nearby. Then, when their belief system is challenged, they have no defense, and they feel like fools. They often end up abandoning the teachings that were given to them when they were children.

Someday your students need to graduate from childhood into young adulthood, and as John writes, "*You do not need that anyone teach you*" (1 John 2:27). Many of our teens are still in spiritual kindergarten. Kindergarten is a great place . . . for children. But imagine trying to keep people penned up in spiritual kindergarten into their adult years!

Spiritual maturing and church attendance are not synonymous. One can attend church several times a week for years and never grow up.

When I was a young youth leader, I didn't get the importance of "self-feeding," the function of the Accountability stage. I continually spoon-fed all my teens with bite-sized tidbits of Scripture without regard to their true spiritual dietary needs. Sometimes youth leaders hesitate to spend much time in Bible study for fear of losing their attention . . . or attendance. If that is the case, one can only imagine why insecure young leaders like me would have shied away from even greater demands that are involved in discipleship.

I wanted the students to like the youth group. After all, how could I minister to them if they didn't? I was hesitant to change their sweet diet, much less hand them a spoon to feed themselves. Too risky. So, during my early ministry years, my young people (like many youths in other groups) graduated and went off to college thinking that their faith was secure.

Then they got slammed.

Our students' faith and values are being challenged at every point, and they feel defenseless. They often conclude that their faith is a nursery school fable or just a ritual for unthinking people. What if we have overlooked an absolutely vital reality, that youth ministry is about helping young believers mature, teaching them how to learn and think for themselves?! That would be a far better approach than for them to forever depend upon others to tell them what to think. The path of discipleship is not easy. It is a road less traveled because, frankly, it is much easier *not* to hold youth accountable.

Accountable? Even that term helps us see why this stage of growth may be the most overlooked step in the growth process in the Church, especially in youth ministry. Frankly, it is not easy.

But the result of not discipling teenagers is tragic. In her book on American teens' faith, Kenda Creasy Dean wrote this: "American young people are, theoretically, fine with religious faith—but it does not concern them very much, and it is not durable enough to survive long after they graduate from high school."[2] Is this reality sobering enough to move us to start discipling our teens as soon as possible? Growth is not a secret in any other arena of life. It is expected.

IT'S NO SECRET . . . THAT THE WORLD NEEDS US TO BE OVERCOMERS

What, then, is the goal of discipling?

For starters, discipleship is not the end goal. It is an intermediate step toward a larger goal: leading young believers to become not just disciples, but disciple makers. That would be the next stage, Ability. Simply put, the goal of this middle stage is to develop strong followers of Jesus who reflect God's character into the world and push back against the evil one. One important aspect of this stage is to help students move from spoon-feeding to self-feeding. But then, we also hope they will truly be prepared for the final stage of maturity: spiritual leadership. That stage is spiritual "Ability," and it is about discipling others.

Small group Bible study is a good place for new believers to start their faith journey. Small groups should help develop their *love* for the Master. Discipleship moves us beyond those first baby steps in the Faith to become self-disciplined *learners* who can appreciate and digest the meat of the Word that will prepare them for combat. Mentoring, the last phase of our maturing process following discipleship, moves us from learning to *leading*. Discipleship is in the middle of the multi-stage process as we move from lovers of the Word to learners of the Word to leaders of the Word!

First, we are being fed. Then, we become self-feeding. Lastly, we begin to feed others. The Church—and the world—are waiting for us to get with it! It is no secret that the world is desperately in need of the hope we have in Christ. Our young people should become spiritually prepared for that great rescue operation.

IT'S NO SECRET ... THAT DISCIPLESHIP WORKS!

I know. You wouldn't expect me to have written a whole book about discipleship if I didn't think it works. But it does! Jesus modeled it, and then commanded us to follow suit.

The thing is, discipling youth is a dynamic tool for the Kingdom. Admittedly, the process will take time to pay rich dividends. You see, there is a learning curve for every believer, a process in discipling that takes time and effort. Many people today seem to prefer instant and pre-packaged. Discipleship just doesn't fit into that mold.

Yet, any worthwhile undertaking takes time. It must germinate and go through a lot of trial and error. This may seem to take forever. The discipling process takes time to gain traction. As for me, I had to start by reshaping my concept of discipleship.

When I was growing up in my church in central Missouri, we didn't use the word "discipleship." After all, the common wisdom seemed to be that there were only twelve "Disciples" (with a capital "D"), and they had passed from the scene nearly two millennia ago.

That club was sacred . . . and closed. Discipleship was not available to mere church members like me. Somehow, the idea that we were all to be Jesus' disciples just never occurred to me.

Things began to change in my junior year in high school. A new pastor came to our church. He was different. I was so intrigued with this young seminary student. He actually seemed to *like* Jesus. He talked freely about disciples as if anyone could be one! Through his patient conversations with me beyond youth group meetings, I began to change my mind about Jesus.

Later, in my first full-time ministry after college at Calvary Church in downtown Kansas City, I began a stumbling effort to disciple students. My first "discipleship" effort was a rather awkward growing process. One young man named Curt met with me regularly for several months. We read and discussed some books together, but I confess the effort was a bit fumbling.

When I moved to Maywood Church, I began to disciple students more intentionally. I also met other churches' youth leaders who had the same interest that I did in moving youth ministry forward into more effective discipling. Tony Dyer, who served at a nearby church, was the primary organizer of an event he called "Disciple Now." We all learned together. It was definitely a work in progress; I learned lots . . . over time.

I admit, I am still learning. But I stay with it. Why? Because after those initial faltering steps, I began to see the incredible rewards that came from discipling young people.

And so will you.

Sadly, discipleship may be a secret to many in youth ministry. But it wasn't a secret to Jesus, who discipled young people who would later change their world. Amazing things are possible among your young people. Discipleship is the key. But it remains a secret to many.

It doesn't need to be a secret to you. Don't let discipleship scare you. Hold your nose and dive in. Commit to the long haul, and don't give up if things feel clunky in the beginning. It may be a long journey, but no one wants to look back and regret that we didn't take the road less traveled!

CHAPTER 3

DEFINING DYNAMIC DISCIPLESHIP

Clearing Up Misconceptions

Spiritual growth is not automatic. Surprised? Probably not. But this seems to be the assumption in many churches. We seem to believe that church members will inevitably grow as they participate in worship, hear sermons, etc.

Look around. In many churches, it's just not happening.

If we hope to accomplish Jesus' Commission in Matthew 28:18-20 to "*make disciples of all nations*," then perhaps we will need to elevate discipleship from its current overlooked and under-rated status to one that is critical to the Church's mission. Discipleship is rooted in Scripture as perhaps the most central function of ministry, especially with young people.

After all, what is the goal for spiritual children? Don't we desire that they learn to walk on their own and not need to be carried? We want them to become self-disciplined and to experience a fruitful spiritual life. But this does not seem to be happening on a wide scale in youth ministry.

Some people believe discipleship is happening in their church. But what are the results? Recently, a youth pastor told me he is very into discipleship. When I asked him how he disciples his teens, he replied, "Oh yeah, we disciple all our teens at our midweek (attractional style) meetings in their small groups." So, even his lost kids were being "discipled?" Definitions, please!

If you research the word discipleship, you will find dozens of definitions. In a Discipleship.org blog, Justin G. Gravitt wrote this:

> "To sum up, disciple making is a specific type of relationship that is carried out by people who are primarily motivated by Christological, covenantal, or missional aims; they use Jesus' methods that are relational, intentional, and missional, and it leads to fruit that multiplies in the form of new disciples, new disciple makers, and three-dimensional momentum."[3]

While everything in that description is true, I wonder how we might make this concept more suited to the teens in our youth ministries. So . . . what is it?

DISCIPLESHIP DEFINED . . . POORLY

How would Jesus define discipleship? Is it possible that some well-meaning leaders have a fuzzy concept of discipleship? Churches' definitions of discipleship are all over the map. Very often, it seems that discipleship is more like a catch-all for just about everything we might identify as spiritual. Does any and every moment we open a Bible or talk about God in a group constitute discipleship? Perhaps it would be helpful to define discipleship first by explaining what it is NOT! Let's explore how discipleship is more than the following concepts below.

Discipleship is MORE THAN a Youth Ministry "In-Group"

Just because a youth leader holds a Bible study for students in his home, this does not in and of itself constitute discipleship. A youth leader's small inner group may pick up some pointers by spending extra time with him or her, but this would not automatically rise to the level of discipleship. Proximity to a youth leader does not, by itself, constitute discipleship.

Discipleship is MORE THAN Sunday School or a Small Group

In a healthy youth group, members will not all be at the same place along the journey toward spiritual maturity. We would probably all agree that small groups provide a good starting point for spiritual Equipping. But in a small group setting, real Accountability is missing. Students may come and go at will. If that is discipleship, where is the discipline?

It is a mistake to try to make everyone in the youth group participate together in disciple training. That may sound elementary to you, but it wasn't so obvious to me as I began my journey. I learned the hard way that I could not expect everyone in my youth group to want the solid food of God's Word. Hebrews 5:12–14 indicates that milk precedes meat.

I even tried to convert our Sunday school program into discipleship. Which only demonstrated that I did not understand the true nature of discipleship. Many students who showed up were there for reasons other than spiritual hunger.

Discipleship is MORE THAN a Second Sunday School

Please hear this! You certainly do not want to offer your youth a little more of the same thing and call it discipleship! As they grow, they desire to leave behind the spiritual Gerber's to pursue real meat. Discipleship is not about the greater quantity of intake of the same baby food.

I mean, do you really have the time to do the same kind of thing with the same people several times a week? Is this the best use of your time? Wouldn't it be better to use some of your valuable time for a step-up experience for youth who are ready for some spiritual steak?

Discipleship is MORE THAN a Class or a Deeper Academic Exercise

Allow me to add one more nuance to address the idea that discipleship is just more Bible study. Sometimes disciple leaders attempt to go beyond an additional "Bible study light" by demanding that students dig deeper, study harder, and even engage in memorizing Scriptures. This, to them, satisfies the definition of discipleship.

But, while deeper study of Scripture and memorizing are a valuable part of discipleship, it simply cannot be limited to these disciplines alone! Real discipleship involves on-the-job training. It is active and dynamic, and it involves more than getting together to study Scripture, in-depth though it may be. Thus, we should never present discipleship to students as some sort of class that they take, and afterward, they can put the books aside, hang the certificate on their wall, and declare themselves *bona fide* disciples of Jesus. Is discipleship a class? Really?

Nah! Actually, should we even use the word class when we talk about discipleship? I submit to you that this is not motivating enough for most people, but especially not for teens.

Can you imagine Jesus' ministry being successful had He told the disciples, "Hey, I'm going to meet you at the synagogue for an hour each week. Bring a quill and scroll, and I will have some study materials for you. We will fill in the blanks together."

Huh?

Does this sound exciting? Life changing? World-shaking? Hardly. That sort of classroom-style approach is unappealing to most of us, but especially to the young men and women who are craving firsthand, action-oriented life application of biblical principles.

Those first disciples were not drawn to Jesus because they were hoping for another Bible study. They were attracted by the energy, passion, and purpose of Jesus and wanted to be part of *whatever* He was up to. They knew that no matter what else they might encounter on the journey ahead, boredom would not be on board!

Discipleship is not merely about learning more Scripture, even as important as that is. It is about much, much more. There is a much more exciting destination!

DISCIPLESHIP'S TRUE DESTINATION

If discipleship is to attract young people, they will need a highly motivating goal. What, then, would actually motivate teenagers to attempt something that goes way beyond normal youth group activities? Why would anyone seek self-discipline? Donald Whitney opens his book *Spiritual Disciplines for the Christian Life* with this equation: "Discipline without direction is drudgery."[4] There must be a destination! Where are we going? Will the destination be worth it?

From the very first paragraphs of this book, we have identified our destination: Jesus Himself. There is no other place to begin than with the desire to know Jesus personally and intimately. At the Global Institute, we call it "chasing after Jesus!" That may not sound too sophisticated or even theologically palatable, but it is a metaphor we use to encapsulate the essence of what it means to be a disciple. Jesus' invitation? "Follow me." The result? "I will make you fishers of men." To those first disciples, being a disciple of Jesus was an adventure . . . the greatest adventure.

Does discipleship sound boring to your teens? Then perhaps it is because they have not truly seen the exciting destination, Jesus! Can anyone show me the Bible verse where it states that someone— anyone—followed Jesus and got bored? Then what is it about the picture of Jesus we present to teens that makes them yawn?

Since we cannot assume that spiritual growth is automatic, perhaps we should consider what motivates anyone to pursue spiritual disciplines. Before most teenagers are willing to pay a price for something, they will first want to visualize the prize. Any coach in any sport understands this. Participants want to know what they are paying a price for. Will it be worth it?

We must give our students something to coax them out of the nest, something that makes it worthwhile for them to venture out of its warmth and safety. They must have a very attractive prize dangled in front of them to help them take the difficult steps toward maturity. Why? Because Accountability can be challenging and even difficult. After all, we are training young disciples to *overcome the evil one*" (1 John 2:14). Does that sound easy or casual? Probably just the opposite. They need to see a prize that makes them salivate!

The prize? To be so close to Jesus that we become *dangerous* to the Devil and disastrous to his evil designs on the human race. Think about it: do football players who are sweating on the practice field do that just for fun? Or do they work out and practice because they dream of becoming champions? Overcomers?! They want to be dangerous! Like a boxer in the ring, they want the opposition to be extremely nervous to face them and deal with their competency.

Discipleship may sound more storybook than real when we talk about Jesus and His disciples, but the truth of the matter is that being a disciple means engaging in hard work and taking some big risks. Sometimes we have handled young people with proverbial kid gloves because we did not want to chase them away with unpleasant sounding words like "study" or "discipline." But, trust me, they know instinctively that winning involves working.

Below is the definition that we have embraced as we disciple teens, based on 1 John 2:12-14. It includes the who, the what, and the why of discipleship:

*"A disciple is one who is surrendering to the Spirit
and accountable to a more mature saint to develop
self-disciplined <u>character</u>, Scriptural <u>confidence</u>, and servant leader <u>competence</u>, in
order to engage in disciple making."*

It will take the rest of this book to lay out all that is involved in that definition! But hang on! First, let's explore two reasons why any teenager would desire to follow Jesus as a disciple.

DISCIPLESHIP'S DYNAMIC DUO

This is where we come into the picture. There are two very practical motivations that will help a young person truly desire to follow Jesus as a disciple. These two motivations may surprise you. Paul wrote about them in 2 Timothy 2:2, to remind Timothy that ". . . *the things you have heard me say in the presence of many witnesses entrust to reliable people who will also be qualified to teach others.*" The two important motivations, the "dynamic duo" for self-discipline, are these:

- First, they look ahead to learn from significant role models who follow Jesus.
- Later, they look behind them to lead others in strategic ministry to follow Jesus.

I'm sure you may be wondering what is so motivating or dynamic about those two things. Let's take a closer look at what Scripture tells us will motivate our young people to become disciples.

First Motivation: Learn from Significant Role Models who Follow Jesus

Everyone learns from someone. In fact, we watch others more closely than we realize to try to figure out life. Most especially, we watch people whom we respect. Young people turn to adults for guidance. They learn from parents, coaches, teachers, pastors, and club or team leaders.

If you are a youth leader, your first challenge may be to disciple adults who will be future disciplers among your young people. Your ministry will grow, and you will need help.

Paul knew this. He first discipled young Timothy and encouraged him to follow "*the pattern of sound words which you have heard from me, in faith and love which are in Christ Jesus*" (2 Timothy 1:13). Tim would later disciple many others. Young people may idolize movie actors, sports figures, and music stars, but they will truly listen to adults in their lives who love and care for them, as Paul loved Timothy like a son. They crave approval from these valued elders.

Yet, many adults do not think of themselves as potential role models to anyone, much less teenagers. "Who, me? A discipler? With teenagers? You've got to be kidding, right?" They do not think of themselves as educated enough, or polished enough, or "hip" enough, or, well, you name it. The reality, however, is that young people in our churches are starving for attention from significant adults in their lives.

Most adult believers can (and should) be disciplers. In the book, *What I Wish My Youth Leader Knew About Youth Ministry,* Mike Nappa described how students were surveyed about the qualities they look for in a youth leader. Guess what: age was a non-factor. It didn't matter to the students how old their adult leader was. Coolness was not a factor, either. The biggest desire of students was this: Does this leader have a genuine love for Jesus and for students like me?[5] Parents, mature college students, and volunteer adult leaders *can* be disciplers with proper training. Why? Because they are already significant to teenagers by being caring adult believers.

Having said that any believer has potential to be a role model, shouldn't we dig deeper into what kind of person teens would really be drawn to? I would suggest that the first qualification for a discipler is this: something in a disciple leader's life must attract followers, you know, like a magnet. A discipler must be headed somewhere in life with an intentionality and passion that is worth following. A potential discipler must be a bit farther down the road toward an attractive, real, and discernible goal of spiritual fulfillment in Christ, making teenagers salivate for whatever it is that energizes this person.

Clearly, Jesus attracted the Twelve like a spiritual magnet; they were intrigued by His life and message. What attributes would attract prospective disciples to a discipler? These would likely make the list:

- Scriptural appetite: Adults are magnetic who are enthusiastic and consistent about personally learning from God's Word.
- Answered prayer: Adults who can relate direct answers to prayer will attract teens who want to know why this adult's prayers are more effective than their sometimes empty or ineffective prayers.
- Ability to fight off the enemy: This is closely linked to both Scripture and prayer and refers to the will to keep rising even when knocked down by enemy attacks. Why? Because overcoming is possible. And worth the effort.
- Effective Evangelism: Adults whose walk overflows into sharing Christ with others become magnets to believers who want to know how that is done because it produces fulfilling fruit.
- Meaningful Body life engagement: Adults who go above and beyond the call of duty to invest in the life of the congregation have credibility with young people. Attending worship only but not shouldering the load lends little credibility among teens.

These are the kinds of qualities that draw spiritually hungry youth to significant role models. A person need not seem to be spiritually perfect to be a discipler. However, disciplers must be far enough out front that they stand out as someone worth following. They must have demonstrated the capacity to overcome the evil one themselves. They are focused on the goal and making progress to achieve it! They serve as magnets to young people because of their overcoming faith.

Maybe you have had an experience like this: It happened to me at the conclusion of a Vacation Bible School for the younger teens in our church. A young man came up to me and asked to speak to me. We went to a corner of the room; I can still vividly remember the exact spot. He said, "I just want you to know how much I love you." (He paused for a moment; do you realize how difficult it must have been for a fourteen-year-old guy to say that?)

Then he said, "There are three people in the world who are heroes to me. The first is Jesus, the second is my dad." After a pause, he said, "And the third is you." He hugged my neck and walked out of the room, leaving me stunned.

You see, I had thought that the week was a waste . . . you know how some teen events can be . . . and then this amazing young man tells me that I am his hero. Whoa! Get outta' town!

The point? I felt like a failure that week. But this young man saw in me the desire to overcome, to plow through difficulties toward a worthy goal . . . to reach him and his peers with the hope of Christ! Good disciplers are not perfect; they just get back up after perceived failures. They don't quit. They are motivated by an objective so great that it causes them to keep moving forward.

Second Motivation: Lead Others in Strategic Ministry to Follow Jesus

A huge oversight in many discipleship programs is the lack of a plan for what follows after the discipleship experience. Discipleship is about learning to become something, to do something truly worthwhile, to pass along something valuable to others. But, in many cases, it is almost as if discipleship is a "course," an end in itself. What is the purpose of being discipled if it is not to utilize that training for some worthy purpose? It has been said that discipleship's purpose is to "develop fully devoted followers of Jesus." Okay, yes. But doesn't this imply that you would want to become like Him, moving forward to do what He did, serving as He served, changing lives . . . and the world . . . as He did? If that is so, then shouldn't it be assumed that those we disciple would bravely follow Jesus to do what Jesus did . . . minister to the lost and disciple the saved? At some point they would hope to have a significant impact as Jesus works through them to touch the lives of others.

We often asked incoming Global Institute interns why they chose to be with us. Predictably, their answer was "to learn."

Nope.

Then I would explain, "You are not here to learn." That came as a bit of a surprise to many. Then I told them, "You got it half right. You are here to learn . . . to lead." Discipleship is not inwardly focused; in fact, its ultimate goal is outwardly focused on spiritual multiplication.

And who doesn't want to live a life of significance? Does anyone truly desire to be overlooked, unnoticed, unimportant? We are born with a God-given desire to live a life that matters, a life of impact. Larry Crabb, in his book *Understanding People*, wrote of our deep-seated need for impact. "Relationship and impact: legitimate thirsts of the human soul. . . . We long to minister to others. We feel whole and good when we do. Ministry satisfies our longing for impact."[6]

Our disciples have observed us, trusted us, and joined with us to chase after Jesus because they admired our determination to do the same.

When students are enlisted for discipleship, it should be made clear to them that the end objective is not only to become Equipped to stand strong in their faith. They will also someday be able to share what they have learned, hopefully with unbelievers who then become believers who actually desire to follow in their footsteps as valiant overcomers. The goal here is that disciples will become godly influencers in the lives of younger believers coming up behind them.

This became a reality for us only a couple of years into our discipling experience. The younger students greatly admired the increasing boldness and spiritual confidence they observed in the older students who were chasing after Jesus. The older students were somewhat unaware of their magnetic influence among the students. Their focus was on following Jesus.

We were at camp when some of the older guys grabbed me to pray with them over some of their lost friends. We had found a side room to start a prayer circle when two little middle-school boys came busting in. When they saw the older guys, they froze in terror. Then Gary, a senior, said, "Join us for prayer, guys!" The little boys were horrified. But what ya gonna do? The big guys were telling these boys to join them! Was there a choice? During the prayer, not a peep from those two. After the prayer time ended, these little guys bolted for the exit like lightning.

But while we were grabbing our Bibles to go to worship, one of the little guys returned. He came up behind Gary and tapped him on the shoulder. "Can I tell you something?" Gary was like, "Yeah, dude." He said, "When I grow up, I want to be just like you." Then he bolted . . . again, blowing out the exit like a maniac. Gary was clearly reeling. He turned to me and said, "Did you hear what he just said to me?" Of course, I did, but asked, "What did he say?" Gary repeated what the little guy had said. Then he mused, sort of to himself, "Man . . . I've got to change!" Yep, that's what I'm talking about. He got it. God was using his influence to motivate those coming behind him. For that reason, he would need to continue his upward trajectory to become more and more like Jesus . . . and in so doing, become more and more the example to others that they so desperately desire and need.

DISCIPLES REACH BOTH BEYOND AND BEHIND

Paul wrote in 2 Timothy 2:2 that discipleship must involve reaching ahead to someone beyond us spiritually, as Timothy followed Paul. But it also must reach back to bring along those who are coming up behind us. Together, these two aspects of discipleship will motivate disciples to keep chasing after that holy ambition.

Hopefully, by now you have agreed that we must not allow spiritual children to remain at the baby level for too long. Our objective should be to move them toward spiritual Accountability as intentionally as possible. Instead, in many churches, spiritual children have never been exposed to spiritual disciplines. Then we wonder why they seem so needy and spiritually anemic as adults.

When we allow that, we have cheated them of spiritual strength. We have crippled the Church by failing to produce a new generation of spiritual warriors. We have forfeited the battlefield because we didn't even lead the soldiers into the epic fight against the evil one.

Nobody wins in this scenario . . . except for the Devil himself.

The single (and Scriptural) solution to this awful "loser scenario" is discipleship done right. Honestly, there is no other route to spiritual maturity. And there is no better way to overcome, to win, to bring light to the darkness, to rescue a lost and dying world other than through discipleship. Discipleship should be done and done with intentionality.

Can you think of another way? An easier way? (Please say you do, and then write a book about it. I'll be first in line to buy that mind-blowing, earth-shattering treatise!)

But, if not, then get ready to jump in.

Oh, wait! Just before you do, perhaps it would be good to take time to explore a few details that will help you start out smart! That is the subject of Part Two.

PART TWO

STARTING OUT SMART

Discipleship Details

CHAPTER 4

WHY DISCIPLESHIP ISN'T DONE. . .

And What You Should Do About It!

My guess? This may well be the chapter where you are most tempted to put this book down and step away from discipleship. Why? Because even though discipleship is the secret ingredient to dynamic youth ministry, many leaders detour around it. You probably already know the reason: discipleship done right can be demanding. This is why you and those who may choose to become part of your discipleship team must carefully consider the costs in advance. Even a novice discipler would acknowledge this reality. In the interest of full disclosure, let's examine at least the primary reasons why discipleship is not done. Better yet, what you can do about it in order to be prepared in advance. That way, when you start, you can start smart!

TO START SMART, RE-EDUCATE YOUR STUDENTS (AND PARENTS)

Before they became the Twelve, the first disciples were only followers of Jesus (Availability stage) who had no responsibility for ministry. They were participants only. They showed up as they wished. But when they became His disciples, they became accountable to Jesus 24/7. They submitted to His leadership and His discipline. It was all-in or all-out. Costly stuff. Let's explore some (not all) of the costs of discipleship, the Accountability stage, for teens.

It May Involve the Sacrifice of Other Pursuits

You may need to re-educate some teens (and their parents) about the true nature of discipling. There is an idea floating out there that participation in church endeavors should not be costly or restrictive. Church activities should be free and available to all without discrimination, limitations, or cost.

Hogwash.

For your students, being discipled will involve a time commitment that will require sacrifice. They may need to curtail (or even give up) some other valuable time commitments in sports, dance team, relationships, or other interests. In fact, I would say that if your discipleship experience requires little sacrifice from students, they will see it as a cheap add-on. If there is no cost, no sacrifice associated with a discipleship ministry, it probably is not true discipleship.

Do you think Jesus' first disciples viewed their commitment as cheap? Hardly! According to Luke 5:11, they *"pulled their boats up on shore, left everything and followed him."* Discipleship, if done biblically, will mean real sacrifice. Students should know this up front! And so should their parents. You will probably need to re-educate everyone when you introduce discipleship.

Carl Trueman wrote that "parents may be culturally authorized to insist that band practice and homework get done. But the same approach to, say, children's prayer or Scripture reading is impossible. That would be shoving religion down their throats."[7]

Now, that is some scary stuff, and some serious re-education will be needed.

Moms have come to me unhappy that their child could not participate in a discipleship group. "How could you keep my son from spiritual growth?" However, it wasn't me who kept the student from discipleship, but rather his own schedule. He worked part-time, played football, and took advanced classes at school. He had no time for discipleship, nor did he indicate that he wanted to make room for it in his already crowded schedule. The mom's idea was that he should be able to attend whenever he was able, and that it was discriminatory and unspiritual to not allow him to participate in discipleship whenever he could squeeze it in.

Can you imagine that same mom telling her son's football coach, "I think you should let my son play football. He won't be able to attend all the practices or learn every play because he is doing so many other important things. But he should play on the team."

I wonder what the coach would say.

Maybe he would say, "Oh, no problem. I didn't understand that he was so busy. Just have him suit up and join us on the field at game time. I'll put him in the game whenever he likes." Not gonna happen.

The mom probably wouldn't dare ask this of the coach. The very idea is ludicrous. But even if she did, the coach would politely inform her that her son could only play if he faithfully attended every scrimmage, practice, and team meeting. Whenever he didn't do these things, he would likely sit on the bench. If that.

I mean, can you even begin to imagine how allowing this would affect the morale and confidence of other players who have sweated in workouts, memorized plays, and spent untold hours preparing for the game? Or how this player could jeopardize their team strategy? Can you visualize the delight of the opposing team at the prospect of placing this clueless player directly in their sights during the game? This kid would put himself and his team in harm's way.

No game for him! Does this seem harsh? Then you would also have to place Jesus in that harsh category. After all, isn't He the one who said to a would-be disciple who wanted first to go bury his father, *"Follow me, and let the dead bury their dead"* (Matthew 8:22)? Does that sound a wee bit harsh? Discipleship is exciting because following Jesus is exciting. But make no mistake: discipleship is to youth group attendance what school sports is to a street lot pick-up game. In discipleship, we are in it to win it. Discipleship is about becoming overcomers in an epic battle against the evil one. Casual commitment? Nah. Re-educate your students and their parents.

It Will Take Personal Effort

Note to self: Discipleship = discipline. Make that *self*-discipline!

Re-education will likely include an evaluation of commitment. If the participants in discipleship are unable to be focused and unwilling to spend the required time learning how to live the Christ-life, then what is the point of discipleship? Why bother? A watered-down approach will produce paltry results, if any. The result of this weak approach to discipleship would be weak believers who think they have been discipled but have nothing to show for it. Instead of moving students toward spiritual maturity and your youth group toward spiritual dynamism, you may have only convinced them that they have attained all that spiritual life offers . . . and it isn't much.

When our students arrived at disciple meetings unprepared with the required Scripture memory or prayer journaling or whatever other items assigned, they were greeted at the door and asked to spend time apart from the group to complete their tasks before joining the others.

We found that if one student could get by with incomplete assignments, eventually that became the new norm for almost everyone. Why should others memorize Scripture and quote it when the leader says to even one disciple member, "Oh, come on in, no problem. Don't worry about your assignment. You can do it later." Yeah, right.

Beyond that, word will get out that discipleship requirements are meaningless. There will be no consequences for negligence or laziness. Students will realize that anyone can be part of your "discipleship" with almost no self-discipline.

Please do *not* water down discipleship. It would be better not to even begin this process than to give students the false idea that discipleship involves little or no discipline.

The end result of such a charade? Your ministry will not produce overcomers who will lead your youth to dynamic youth ministry with amazing displays of the power of God in your community. Forget seeing them lead people to Christ, minister at their schools, or bring glory to God.

Discipleship without accountability is not discipleship because it will lack both discipline and accountability. Go figure!

It Will Require Perseverance

Staying the course may also be an item of re-education for teens. One of the most important keys to effective discipleship is leading the participants to finish what they started. Jesus' disciples sacrificed much to be part of the Twelve. All but one remained faithful to the end. Then, when they became Apostles, they shepherded the expanding Church into the early Church Age. They stayed with it through persecution, abuse, and even to execution. Twenty centuries later, that movement continues. They did not quit. Neither should we.

Your objective is to guide students across that bridge from spiritual infancy into spiritual parenthood. In view of this, you will want to impress upon your discipleship candidates the importance of staying with the group until they graduate from the discipleship ministry, ready to become productive servant leaders and disciplers.

Re-educate your students about the price of discipleship. Let them know the expectations. Full disclosure is vital to your success . . . and theirs.

TO START SMART, REVIEW YOUR PERSONAL SACRIFICE

While discipleship presents an obvious cost for the disciple, it also involves risk and sacrifice by you, the discipler. You are stepping out there by faith, trusting God with your investment of time and energy, and possibly your money. Review these possible costs of discipling students:

Disciplers Pursue Personal Discipline for Themselves

I grew up during a time when discipleship was not a norm in my church. However, when I came to Christ, I started a pilgrimage to learn from Him. I had some help along the way from a caring pastor who discipled me before it was a thing.

Then, when I started working with youth, I instinctively knew that I wanted them to go beyond a passing acquaintance with the Lord. My fervent hope was that they would surrender fully to Jesus as I had when I met Him as a teenager.

One thing I knew for certain: I could not try to disciple anyone who, by watching me, could tell that I was undisciplined in my walk with Jesus. I would have to become an example to them, not by my knowledge alone but by my actions. Spiritually lazy people do not make good disciplers. Is perfection a prerequisite for them? No. But spiritual discipline and effort? Yes. Perfection is not the criterion but honesty and humility plus persistence. Loafers do not make good leaders.

As a discipler, I would first need to be actively involved in personal quiet times, including Scripture study and memorization, and have a healthy prayer life.

Second, I would need to have been engaged in verbal Evangelism and have fruit to show for it—people who have come to faith as the Lord used my testimony by the power of His Spirit.

Last, I would need to be involved in the life of a local congregation, giving effective service beyond what was expected of me. If the discipler is a youth minister, that person would likely go above and beyond their usual paid responsibilities. And volunteer disciplers?

No one is paying them to disciple the youth, after all! Their motivation must come from Somewhere Else.

Disciplers Pay the Price of Scrutiny and the Loss of Privacy

It should go without saying that anyone who leads teenagers should submit to a background check. Beyond that, all disciplers should themselves be accountable to the church's leadership.

And then? Your disciples will also place you under a microscope to be watched constantly. Who wants that? Especially in today's social climate in which everyone thinks that they should be free from scrutiny except in well-crafted social posts. For some disciplers, the greatest cost is the loss of some measure of personal downtime. It's hard to really relax with people watching your every move. You have to be "up" for them, relating to them, looking after their needs. Discipleship, by its nature, is costly because it is an invasion of your privacy. Paul wrote, *"For you yourselves know how you ought to follow our example, because we did not act in an undisciplined manner among you . . . in order to offer ourselves as a model for you, that you might follow our example"* (2 Thessalonians 3:7,9 NAS). Paul knew he was being watched!

When our first overseas Global staff members, Matthew McIntosh and Jamey Dickens, were in training, they stayed at our house. This was before we had a campus of our own to house trainees. They studied in our den, ate with us, and wrestled on our living room floor. Later, at the end of his first year of service in Moldova, Jamey told me, "Sometimes I feel like I am always 'on' with the students here. I can never relax; I have to be vigilant about my example. I have to be intentional about how I spend downtime, time with God, and time with my associates." Uh-huh, welcome to discipleship world. When you disciple others, you will be closely observed.

Disciplers Prepare to Sacrifice Some of Their Personal Time

An inescapable part of your decision to disciple youth will be a determination about the amount of time you will spend on it each week. Frankly, one of the greatest tools in the discipler's toolbox is simply spending time with your disciples. How you choose to use your discretionary time is a part of the equation. Beyond work and family, other time-consumers like church, house upkeep and repairs, recreational activities, and so many other things compete for your time. You are busy. But remember, your time is your investment. How will you use it?

Time is precious. When we invite people into our lives for discipleship, we give them a gift. It is not renewable. Once given, your time cannot be retrieved. Giving students your time is a very real investment, and they know it intuitively. Teenagers know when they are a priority . . . or not. They are keenly aware. Just being there for them is huge. Most of us have heard about spending quality time with people we love. Frankly, in our hurried culture, any time is helpful.

Teens understand that you have time constraints. Even Jesus' disciples did not each get Him all to themselves in measured individual increments of quality time. Of course, they always had access to Jesus, but mostly as a group and in a variety of settings in which His focus was often on other people, even groups of other people. Does that sound like the common definition of quality time?

Students want to know if real Christianity can be lived out in everyday experience. Anyone can put on a show at the church house for an hour or so. But your disciples know that if they get to spend time with you . . . in your normal routine . . . there is something special about that. Not everyone gets to do that. We don't open our homes and invite the whole world to come in and put up their feet in our easy chair, raid our fridge and, in general, act like family. So, when you and I spend extra time with students, we offer them a gift of time and vulnerability that is reserved for a few.

Now, *that* is beginning to look and sound a whole lot more like discipleship the way Jesus did it.

You will probably need to get creative. Students in today's hurried culture may be more satisfied than you think with whatever extra time you can offer them. Even times like when you go fill up your gas tank, or stop by the grocery store, or do other daily tasks. They want time with you. How do they get that? Often, it is just about you being with them and available to them. Think of ways to combine discipling with tasks and recreational interests that you already fit in to your schedule. For example, why not take your group fishing, if fishing is what you enjoy?

In a later chapter, we will discuss in more detail how many weeks or months it really takes to disciple teenagers. For now, let me assure you that the issue is more about realigning your time than about spending huge additional increments of time with student disciples. As Mike Breen pointed out in *Building a Discipling Culture*, "It doesn't have to mean more work; it means we are more efficient and smart in how we use our time."[8] Maybe we should be thinking about more intentionality, not just more time! What it comes down to is the management of time.

TO START SMART, REVISE THE WEEKLY SCHEDULE

Let's make an important clarification about the discipleship schedule. This second growth stage, Accountability, will not replace your disciples' normal youth ministry involvement. But it will add at least one extra weekly meeting to their schedule. Later, it will be the participants' choice to give even more time to include evangelistic or other ministry activities, mostly on their own during routine activities. Our hope is that they will desire this self-discipline.

Why only one extra weekly group meeting? Because the discipleship students will also be expected to plan, participate in, and probably help with the regular Availability level youth activities. Just as Jesus' disciples helped Him with His many ministry activities, your disciples will do the same. It is important to remember that they are not leaving the regular weekly Availability level programming but learning to assist with it. They are, however, adding one other weekly time with you and other disciples, separate from regular youth meetings.

Realign Your Time to Concentrate on What Matters

It took a while, okay years, for me to realize that if I spent all my time with all the youth, I would then have little or no time left to invest in a few future young leaders. I was programming every event to involve every youth every time we met. This was very short-sighted of me. I needed to always keep in view where I hoped our youth ministry could be in one or more years, not just this week. So long as today—and all the teens right in front of me—was my primary (read: only) focus, that almost guaranteed that five years from today my ministry would probably look just like today.

Is that what any of us really want? The same kids at the same spiritual level for their whole experience in the youth ministry? But if I apportion my time and invest some of it wisely in future leaders, there is the real possibility that with time, my youth group can truly soar!

TO START SMART, REFOCUS ON FUTURE SUCCESS!

So, now you know. Discipleship very often isn't done because discipleship, when done right, is tough. It is tough on your young disciples because when they choose to chase after Jesus, they will be stretched and tested like never before.

It is also tough on you as the leader because you must hold your disciple students accountable. Often, they think they want this until they actually get it. Then they are not quite so sure. And you get to be the bad guy who demands increasing self-discipline from them.

You will need to refocus from the price to the prize—spiritually mature overcomers—throughout this process. You must see the disciples not as they are, but as they will be by God's grace. Sometimes that objective will take longer than you expected and will become reality much later than you hoped. If you cannot visualize the result of your labor from the beginning, you may find yourself tiring of the effort. When you don't see quick results, or you get pushback from your disciple students, or your other obligations seem to be faltering, then you will need to have the glorious end in mind. Otherwise, you may cave to discouragement and choose to quit.

Just keep focusing on the future, the possible prize! Picture the wins!

When all is said and done at the end of your journey in life, it will not be the money in the bank or the large house or the trophies in your study that will matter. The trophies may well be discarded. The money will move to someone else's accounts. The house will be sold, updated, and eventually torn down to make way for bigger or better.

But what will last, and even be passed on to generations until Jesus returns, will be the fruit of your investment in other people's lives. That legacy will be the rich source of tales told in Heaven! Not to mention your Master's approval. Face it: approval from a highly authoritative source is what we all crave to the core of our being. Imagine hearing this from our Father in Heaven (the Ultimate Authority): "Well done, good and faithful servant."

While standing before a group of young people to speak, I often ask the Lord, "What am I looking at here?" I have learned to look past their exterior or I will miss what God sees, which is often way deeper than what I initially observe. 1 Samuel 16:7 reminds us, *"The Lord does not look at the things people look at. People look at the outward appearance, but the Lord looks at the heart."*

Ben was a spunky seventh grader when I first "saw" him. He had started out with a very inconsistent attendance. But I talked with him often and personally invited him to come to this or that event.

Years later, after he had gone away to an out-of-town university, he wrote me a letter. In it he reminded me of the personal attention which I had given him as a thirteen-year-old. For him, this had an impact I had never realized. He wrote that were it not for that personal recognition, he probably would never have become involved in the youth group, much less a leader of it, and certainly would not have dedicated his life to service in missions abroad!

Who knew that he would later impact the lives of many people? I could have missed him. But the Lord wants us to see what He sees.

Maximus, the gladiator in the movie by that name, told his soldiers that their efforts would "echo in eternity." Your earthly effort will last for eternity; it will be recorded—and recounted—in the halls of Heaven. Forever. Keep the worthy prize in view!

So, are you in? Later, in Part Three on Equipping, we will begin to tackle the ingredients of successful Accountability ministry with young people through discipleship. But before we do that, let's explore the enlisting process, and how to start out smart…with the right people. Buckle up. There could be some turbulence ahead.

CHAPTER 5

MAKING DISCIPLESHIP DOABLE RIGHT FROM THE START

How to Find the Right People to Disciple

Now that I have given you several reasons why many would not even attempt to engage young people in discipleship, let me offer a word of hope: discipleship is incredibly rewarding (and fun)! Rather than adding it as a duty, another meeting, or even a new organization, perhaps it would be better to think of discipleship as organic, simple, and relational. Jesus seemed to view discipleship as more of an ongoing relationship with a focus on spiritual Accountability.

Discipleship may be costly, but it should not be complex or tedious. In fact, it could be a great joy in your life as you help young disciples grow and overcome! Bottom line: it is difficult to conceive how a youth ministry will ever produce lasting fruit for God's Kingdom without it.

How you begin this process will matter. Selecting the right disciples is important and can be daunting, but it is a big key to success. A forward-thinking discipler is always on the lookout for signs that students may be ready for the next step. Whenever we are with students, our radar will be in search mode to identify those who are growing beyond the spiritual childhood stage.

TO START SMART, RESPECT CHRIST'S PATTERN FOR RECRUITMENT

Where does one even start the process of selecting good discipleship candidates? Is there a practical guide for selecting disciples in today's world? Does Jesus' model work? Let's look at the phases of this process. Some phases may overlap, but they are each important.

1. Inquiry Phase

I couldn't help but notice that Jesus spent private time with the Father in prayer before He chose anyone (Luke 6:12). This is a great place to begin. Do not skip this step. Start on your knees. Ask God for His divine direction in choosing disciples. After all, He has already chosen them! Beyond that, pray a blessing over them even now, before you know who they are. Throughout Scripture, we see fathers speaking a blessing over their children. Jesus would speak to the Father often for His disciples. We should not minimize the importance of prayer for our young charges, before, during, and even after our discipleship time with them.

2. Incentivizing Phase

When Jesus spoke to the crowds, He spoke often of the kingdom of Heaven. He was calling them upward to greater things. Students who enter your youth group as spiritual children need to have their sites lifted. How do you get them to move toward discipleship? My dad used to say, "You can lead a horse to water, but you can't make him drink." Then he added, with a twinkle in his eye, "But you can salt the oats!" The leader's task is to salt the oats, giving teens a taste of Scripture that makes them thirst for much, much more. Jesus made discipleship an attractive pursuit. Likewise, we must create a climate that makes discipleship desirable. Drop hints regularly about the advantages of moving into the next stage. And always be sure to *reward* behaviors you really want *repeated*! I'm a fan of what I call secondary motivation. I have heard that Jewish parents would put honey on the tongue of their babies as they read the Torah to them. Hmmm, that sounds like secondary motivation to me. At our summer camps, we award a silly plastic flamingo (like people plant in their yard) to the most enthusiastic team each day. The teens go crazy for the privilege of carrying that thing around all day. Huh? But it works. Here are some simple ideas to help focus teens on greater growth:

- Publicly praise students who exhibit spiritual disciplines (message notes, Scripture memory, etc.).
- Conduct a "Bible Mania" competition at the end of each lesson and give points to winning teams over a period of time. Develop a plan for a fun award for the winning team at the end of the series.
- Ask for input after a lesson. Ask, "What is your takeaway?" Which students respond to this?
- Offer a candy bar at the end of a lesson to the person who shares an apt take-away.
- Share daily Bible readings online or through an app. See who takes the bait. Regularly text participants in a group text.
- Offer a Scripture memory contest with a prize for the winner.

These things are only a start. But bear in mind: discipleship will start to happen when students want it and want it badly. Whatever your list of qualifications, know this: Jesus was looking for spiritually hungry people to become His disciples. So should we. He made it clear to them that discipleship would involve accepting greater responsibility for their own spiritual growth.

Also, your disciple candidates will need to know that they will be servants who get under the whole youth group to lift it up. So, yes, there will definitely be some heavy lifting ahead.

I've often heard this list of qualifications: people who are faithful, available, and teachable. My own mantra for finding disciples is to "find and feed the hungry." And if I can't find any hungry teens? Well, perhaps that falls on me, as a youth leader, to better understand why. Maybe that calls for prayerful consideration of how to beef up the menu so that those in the youth group who are at the Availability stage will begin to hunger and thirst for more.

3. Information Phase

Jesus was honest with people about discipleship. He carefully explained what was required to follow Him. He said to one rich, young wanna-be in Matthew 19:21, *"Sell what you have and give it to the poor, and you will have treasure in heaven; and come, follow Me."* The young man *"went away sorrowful, for he had great possessions."* What does the next verse say? Did Jesus chase after him, begging him to change his mind? Did Jesus tell him, "I will lower the standard just for you; I will adjust the requirements to make this easier for you! Please stay!"? Nope. That young man wanted something else more than he wanted Jesus. And Jesus respected his decision.

When you decide to begin discipleship, you need to let the whole youth group know what discipleship will look like. This means they need to be aware of both the challenges and the benefits. Jesus first demonstrated discipline in every area of His life publicly before all watching eyes. Would-be disciples knew that they were signing up for a life of discipline, humility, and service. They had heard Jesus speak in the synagogue and by the sea. They knew of His teachings and what the Kingdom should look like in their lives. He didn't pull punches. He told them, *"Foxes have dens and birds have nests, but the Son of Man has no place to lay his head."* (Luke 9:58). Sound casual? Easy? Comfortable?

But Jesus also painted them a picture of a fulfilling future: "Follow me and I will make you fishers of men!" Give your youth group—especially prospective disciples—all the facts in advance, both pros and cons. The prize must be worth the price! Describe the discipleship opportunity so everyone can understand what is involved. You want them to know what they are signing up for with as much detail as possible so they will choose you before you choose them.

I know, I know, this sounds very backward. Shouldn't it be the other way around? Jesus chose the disciples, right? Well, yes. But Jesus didn't always choose the obvious candidates. No way. Look at them. Tax collectors? Roughhewn, uneducated fishermen? Kids?

Still, they had one thing in common: they wanted what Jesus offered. He chose them not because they were wealthy, status-conscious, or rabbinically trained, but because they sought Him. In John 1, John and Andrew actually chased after Jesus! Those two disciples were Available. Jesus' first disciples may have seemed a bit dense at times, but they were eager to learn.

Yes, Jesus chose His disciples, according to Mark 3:13–19. But in a very real sense, the disciples chose Him because they hung around, desired to learn more, and had a hunger for spiritual things. This is the kind of young person a youth pastor prays for! But be sure of this: if you don't satisfy this hunger, it may diminish or lead students to seek spiritual growth elsewhere.

4. Invitation Phase

Jesus took His time selecting those first twelve disciples. He personally invited those whom He had been observing in the crowd. You will probably want to invite people personally also. Invite all qualifying students to apply. Like Paul, invite them to come and suffer with you for the Gospel (2 Timothy 1:8–9)! This will cull out some who are not serious. But also, be sure they know that the prize will be worth it! Keep painting that picture! Then, after you have invited all who choose to abide by the stipulations to join the group, you are free to seek out specific students to participate. You won't need to hesitate to invite specific people if you've already made a public invitation to all the eligible students. In the end, each student must make a personal decision based on the stated requirements.

5. Interview Phase

After you have invited youth group members to become discipled, then it is time to individually interview students who have applied. This will involve a process to evaluate students' readiness for this commitment. Jesus, of course, already knew. He greeted Nathanael in John 1:47-49 saying, "*Here truly is an Israelite in whom there is no deceit.*" Surprised, Nathanael asked, "*How do you know me?*" Jesus responded, "*I saw you while you were still under the fig tree before Philip called you.*" He probably had heard Nathanael's prayers there. We may be sure He clearly discerned the disciples' readiness. But for us, an interview will be helpful. It is akin to tryouts or auditions for school activities, which most students expect. It may be informal, or you might ask them to complete a written application. Spend time interviewing each candidate. Ask them why they desire discipleship. Review the requirements and help them evaluate their capability to fulfill them. Discuss their other commitments and the discipleship schedule.

Jesus told one would-be disciple, *"Whoever wants to be my disciple must deny themselves and take up their cross daily and follow me"* (Luke 9:23). Self-denial and submission are apt words to describe discipleship. It seems that, to Jesus, discipleship involves discipline. Hmmm.

Be sure to explain the specifics of the commitment. How many weeks or months will this last? How long will the disciple sessions last each week? What outcomes are desired? What will the assignments be? Will students be expected to memorize verses in the Bible, or even a shorter book of the Bible? Make all this clear to everyone before they are accepted into the group. Make sure that everyone who is affected—whether as a participant or the parent who serves as a chauffeur or listens to their student's Scripture quoting, etc.—has agreed to this commitment.

6. Initial Meeting With the Disciple Group

Once you have been through this pre-discipleship process, you are ready to begin. Get the interested students together informally as a group to review the qualifications and commitment level. Use this first meeting as an opt-out moment. Allow them to experience the relationship commitments they are about to agree to at least one time before they look you in the eye to say they are fully committed. This will give students the time to reconsider very early whether they are prepared to follow through with their discipleship agreement. Better to drop out now than in the middle of discipleship later. If you start smart with these initial six phases, the final phase, the "investment phase," will be more rewarding.

TO START SMART, RECOGNIZE COMPLAINTS AND RESISTANCE

As you enlist students, be aware of some possible pitfalls. The following complaints are among the most common objections given by people who are not in favor of discipling teens.

Challenge #1: The Complaint of Favoritism

Sometimes youth leaders are unfairly accused of showing favoritism to certain students. Discipleship, by its nature, involves a degree of exclusivism. But this discipling type of exclusivism is not unfair, nor can it be legitimately called favoritism in any negative sense.

All humans play favorites; there is no way we could be equally involved with all other humans. We simply do not have the hours or energy it takes to spend equal time or be best friends with everyone, not even all church members! We are not physically capable of maintaining the same level of relationship with everyone we know. Only God can do that.

Honestly, we can't avoid playing favorites. You'd better play favorites with your family, right? However, even though you as a youth discipler may become the target of accusations of favoritism, you can avoid a legitimate accusation of selfish favoritism. How? By carefully explaining the program to everyone before you begin. Then invite all qualifying students to participate on the basis that they have agreed to fulfill the requirements.

Challenge #2: Parental Concerns

Parental support for discipling is so important. Ideally, we would prefer that every parent be their child's discipler. However, we have already observed how parents can sometimes question discipleship because of the time commitment. The protest? Discipleship asks too much of their students who have a heavy schedule with many other activities. They want church activities to be offered as a side dish on the menu.

Even so, I was unprepared for yet another type of objection from parents. And no, I'm not talking about unsaved or unchurched parents who resented the time their student was spending away from home. I'm referring to good church families whose lack of enthusiasm bordered on outright resistance. Parents should be very involved in discipling their teens. Instead, sometimes parents fear that their students are becoming not just too scheduled, but too spiritual. Hmmm. I've rarely heard parents complain that their students were too studious. Or that their son on the football team was too sports minded.

Why is it that parents worry about their children becoming too spiritual? Most parents want well-rounded students who participate in a variety of things. But this is a very compartmentalized view of life, in which secular events and spiritual pursuits are two separate activities. Of course, balance is a very important consideration. To an extent, this is understandable. However, a strong relationship with God through prayer and His Word should be the foundation for life that permeates all other pursuits. It is not just another additional event or time commitment. Rather, it gives meaning and context to every other aspect of a believer's life. It is interwoven into a believer's activities, schedule, interests, and relationships.

Our relationship with God determines the quality of all other aspects of life. It cannot be compartmentalized. Unfortunately, too many try to make it so. The fact that adults often separate spiritual life from secular life—and I mean adults who have grown up in church—is a dismal reality and has very unfortunate consequences, not only for themselves, but for their children who follow in their footsteps.

So, don't be surprised or discouraged if you encounter this attitude from parents and other gatekeepers. You should probably expect it. It will be your privilege to help both parents and students to distinguish between these two very different approaches to life. Either they will continue to insist that "church stuff" is just one of their child's many good but compartmentalized activities, *or* they will agree that their students should learn how to follow Jesus first in every single aspect of their lives. Then, and only then, will every other pursuit find meaning and fulfillment through Him.

We noted that there are three essential discipleship relationships. Ultimately, discipleship is about how we relate as humans with God, a lost world, and the Church. So, in the next chapter, let's put relationships front and center.

CHAPTER 6

DISCIPLESHIP RELATIONSHIPS

How to Develop a Practical and Relational Approach

So, here we are. We have made the big leap into the often-overlooked practice of discipling students. We have carefully chosen willing student participants. And we have held our initial meeting to get acquainted and to review the process and plans for discipleship.

Hopefully, the students now have a clear picture of what is expected and the desired outcomes of discipleship. They know there will be a lot of work involved. Still, they have heard Jesus calling them to become His disciples. They are sitting in your living room waiting for what's next. So. . . what *is* next?

Well, what's next is the seventh and final phase of discipleship—the investment phase—over the course of several months or even longer. Bear in mind that because discipleship is relational rather than transactional, this will probably be messy. Not only will every disciple group be unique, but also every disciple. Relationships are not built assembly line style. We humans are not machines that can be perfectly put together on an assembly line.

START SIMPLY: EMBRACE THREE ESSENTIAL RELATIONSHIPS

In my book, *Youth Ministry by The Book*, I recalled how I once attended a youth leader training event in which the speaker listed 31 things that I needed to do to be successful. I almost quit my position that day. Thankfully, I stumbled across Ephesians 4:11-13 soon after that. In verse 12, Paul outlined only three essential relationship areas for leaders to concentrate on as the basis for guiding young believers: "*To equip his people for works of service, so that the body of Christ may be built up.*" This passage points to three essential relationships for believers:

- Equipping: "*to equip his people*" (leaders help believers to strengthen their relationship with the Master by His Spirit). This relationship is the first and Great Commandment (Matthew 22:37-38) to love God above all things.
- Evangelizing: "*for works of service*" (disciples learn to serve people and build relationships beyond the church doors in the marketplace and wherever possible to ultimately reach a lost world). This relationship is not optional; it is, after all, Jesus' Great Commission (Matthew 28:18-20).
- Encouraging: "*so that the body of Christ may be built up*" (disciples develop relationships with members of the Body to carry out this epic rescue operation). This is the Great Community (John 13:34-35).

Discipleship must embrace these three special kinds of relationships; it is not merely a program. Rather, it is a life practice in which we focus upward in our relationship with God, outward to our relationship with a lost world, and inward with our relationship to the Body of Christ.

Let's take a closer look at these three all-important and essential relationships and how they inform and shape our discipleship efforts. This will be our discipleship template.

First, We Begin by Equipping Disciples in Their Relationship With Jesus

We begin with this first injunction, "*to equip his people. . . .* " Of course, Equipping implies that we are preparing disciples for a task. But Equip how? Are we to teach Bible study techniques? Witnessing skills? Servant roles in the church? Well, of course these things are important. But isn't there something more basic than this in our Equipping task? Yes. There is.

Our first and foremost responsibility as disciplers is to help young people become Equipped with a rich and satisfying friendship with Jesus, the author and finisher of their faith. This is the Great Commandment, given to us by Jesus in Matthew 22:37-38. It is God Himself who desires a personal relationship with each of us. He gives us our very identity.

How do we Equip young disciples to relate properly to God? He has given us two provisions by which we believers may develop our friendship with Him. Our Equipping will focus on these two Spirit-led resources: Scripture and prayer, the two communication tools by which we may relate to God. All relationships involve two-way communication, both listening and speaking. This is also true with our relationship with God. Scripture is God's means of communicating with man. Prayer is God's provision for man to speak freely with Him. Scripture and prayer are simply the biblical descriptions of our two-way communication with God.

As we lead our disciples to have a personal friendship with Jesus, we must dive into Scripture study and prayer. Everything else we address in discipling students will rest on this first and foremost Equipping task. The power for abundant life comes from God alone through His Spirit. In Part Three, we will examine the Equipping relationship Jesus modeled with His disciples.

Second, We Guide Them to Move Outward to Evangelizing Relationships

When disciples relate to God personally, they will eagerly respond to His love and grace with grateful obedience! Serving others will naturally flow out from their growing relationship with God. Ephesians 4:12 continues with this second essential relationship, "*works of service.*" Or as the KJV reads, "*for the work of ministry.*" There can be little doubt what this task refers to. Our goal in service is not inward-focused. In fact, it is ultimately outwardly focused beyond the church doors. Everything the Church does in the world should have but one laser-focused goal—it is known as the Great Commission (Matthew 28:18-20); God invites us to join Him in the greatest rescue operation in history . . . to take the Gospel to the whole world.

Evangelism is really about the restoration of all creation, especially His crowning creation, humanity, to reflect the glory of its Maker. This rescue operation requires wisdom and the application of God's power in strategic ways to take back what the Devil has stolen.

Just as Jesus led His disciples to serve a lost and dying world, we must likewise engage our disciples in that critical enterprise. In fact, we cannot hope to win if we are not winning our world to Christ. Evangelism is a vital part of discipleship training. Later, in

Part Four on Evangelism, we will detail how to engage our disciple students in fruitful witness relationships.

Third, We Nurture Encouraging Relationships Within the Body

The final relationship our disciples must embrace is with the Body of Christ, the Church. Ephesians 4:12 ends with this imperative: "*So that the body of Christ may be built up.*" This third relationship is with fellow believers as part of the Great Community. Thankfully, we don't have to function alone, but within a fellowship of believers, just as the early Church did.

Both Evangelism and Encouraging have the same ultimate objective. While one focuses outwardly to overcome the enemy and rescue the perishing, the other focuses inwardly to ensure that our fellow rescuers are strong and effective together to achieve that singular mission.

It is here, in this eternal fellowship, that we find fulfilling relationships, just as God ordained for us. He designed us to reflect His nature: He is relational. In the Church, we find fulfilling relationships just as God has within the Trinity. In discipleship, your students will also develop relationships with others as they Evangelize their lost acquaintances (Part Four) and then Encourage believers within the fellowship (Part Five). Equipping prepares them for their mission outside the Church and ministry inside the Church.

START STRATEGICALLY: EXPECT A LONGER PROCESS

Ephesians 4:11 identifies spiritual fathers who lead in the Equipping effort: *"So Christ himself gave the apostles, the prophets, the evangelists, the pastors and teachers."* God has provided leaders (all called but not all necessarily vocational) to help teach believers the three essential relationships listed in verse 12. We briefly addressed how discipleship will involve more of your weekly time in Chapter 4. But how many weeks or months will the process take? Let's explore what it takes to produce results in discipleship, whether as a vocational leader or as a volunteer.

The Overall Discipling Duration

I want to reassure you: I have not read anywhere that discipleship requires you to forsake your day job and invite people to live with you for three years, commune-style, so that you may spend all your time with them. Okay? But having said that (you knew the "but" was coming, right?), recognize that discipling is up close and personal. It is doing life together, spending time in closer proximity with your student disciples. It may take longer than, say, a semester.

Discipleship involves modeling a lifestyle. That takes time. It means, for example, showing students how to read the Bible, when to read the Bible, and how long to read the Bible. Frankly, they will probably need to observe it in your own life, and then see the results it produces. If they are to be truly motivated to be more involved in personal Bible study and prayer, it will more likely come because they observed you than because you instructed them.

Let's pose this question in a different way: How long will it take to fully engage your disciples in the three essential relationships? To change the whole world, Jesus spent 24/7 with His disciples for three years. That amounts to 26,280 hours that Jesus spent with those few. How many years would it take, at one hour per week, to approximate that amount of time with a few of your young disciples? Answer: Over 500 years!

If you decide to spend one hour a week for twelve weeks with your disciples—twelve hours total—don't expect them to change the world soon. You will probably be fortunate if you succeed in helping them change even one bad habit or add one good habit. Discipleship is a process that will take time. The longer the duration of your effort, the more likely it is that God can use you to produce life change in the lives of your students and enable them to become world changers. I spent nearly two years during my teen years learning from my church's young pastor. I watched him closely during the many occasions that we were together, whether it was at church, at a youth activity, or on a trip of some kind. I wanted to know how he really lived this Christ-life he embraced so enthusiastically. Still, today in my discipling effort, it seems to take the better part of two semesters—at the very least—to effectively disciple older teens.

Expect a longer duration in order to develop trust. How long will it take for you to build trust that ensures that your disciples will follow your lead in chasing after Jesus? Choose to approach discipling from this perspective. Who knows what could happen if you spent two or more focused hours per week for a few semesters to meet with your disciples? You may greatly increase the potential impact by spending more than a dozen sessions with them.

START SMALL: ENLIST ONLY A FEW PARTICIPANTS

As we consider time restraints, we naturally wonder how we could come close to the example set by Jesus, given our circumstances. But perhaps smaller is better. We should consider the advantages of smallness when it comes to discipleship, both in people and places.

Fewer is Better

A question that closely follows the issue of time commitment is this; "How many young disciples can I impact rather than merely inform?" Jesus had a handful of disciples, and yes, they were a handful! They were from vastly different segments of society, careers, spiritual backgrounds, and persuasions. They had trouble getting along with each other at times.

Hmmm. If Jesus had twelve disciples (and didn't one of them, Judas, deny Him?), then how many disciples do we think we can handle?

I would probably struggle with even six young people at a time. I'm not trying to set your limits; I'm just thinking of my own limitations. Even while Jesus had the Twelve, He would take three disciples—Peter, James, and John—on separate occasions to pour into them apart from the others. Consider beginning with only a few—maybe three or four—at least in the first stages of your discipling journey. You may choose to take on more in a future disciple team. Start small and aim for quality rather than quantity.

Familiar is Best

Fewer disciples will also enable a wider range of meeting locations. You may think the church house is the best place for your meetings. But shouldn't discipleship take place wherever life happens most of the time for you and them? Where possible, choose smaller and more familiar places for your meetings, like the coziness of a living room or den . . . yours or theirs.

Beyond that, choose a smaller location for activities with disciples. What better location to disciple youth than in homes . . . yours and theirs? Think about how Jesus discipled The Twelve. They learned from Him as He taught the masses, and they learned from Him as He healed people in their own homes. Almost all of these activities were close to home. After all, they are learning how to live the Christ-life, right? They will learn best by watching you practice living the Christ-life in normal daily routines.

When Jesus began His earthly ministry, where did He start? In John 1, we are introduced to Jesus' first followers, who had been followers of John the Baptist. While John was preaching one day, Jesus passed by. He acknowledged Jesus to His followers in verse 36 by saying, "*Behold the lamb of God!*" Those two young men immediately followed Jesus, but from a distance.

Here's the good part: Jesus turned around and confronted them. Can't you just see those two young men back up, startled, as Jesus faced them? He asked, in verse 38, "*What do you seek?*"

Good question! What *did* they seek? Did they want a Sunday school lesson? Did they desire a lecture or a sermon? Maybe just some information? No. We get a hint of what they wanted in their answer: "*Where are you staying?*" These two boys didn't want information; they wanted an *invitation*! They wanted to know where Jesus lived. They wanted to investigate the truth about Him up close and personal.

Your potential disciples want the same thing. They are interested in you, not just what you know. They want to come to your house.

They want to watch how you live. They want to check out your fridge. They want to sit in your easy chair. They want to see your movie collection and music playlists. And speaking of taste, they want to taste (translate: eat all) your food.

They want the real deal.

So, let them come. Let them be underfoot, all up in your stuff. It is there that they will best learn what it means to abide in Christ.

Of course, I am not suggesting that these students come and live with you. I'm not saying you should ignore your family or your work or other pursuits. But—sorry to break it to you—discipleship will clearly be a challenge at times. You will need to set boundaries, but those boundaries will likely be somewhat more inclusive for your disciples than for other acquaintances and even the other youth group members. Your disciples will be more like family.

In fact, even in the early Church, believers met from house to house. What better place than that to begin your discipleship adventure? I don't know where I would be today had it not been for my visits to Brother Gary's home. (We all called him Brother Gary. Don't ask me why.) He was our pastor, but also the youth leader by default; no one else wanted *that* job.

Brother Gary entered my world when I was a teenager. He couldn't have come at a better time, at least for me. I was on my way out. Out of that little central Missouri town. Out of that small town church. Out of all religious affiliations. Out.

But when Gary arrived, he brought Jesus with him. This was a Jesus I had never met; at the very least, it certainly wasn't the Jesus I thought I knew. You have probably heard of him, the somewhat boring, distant, legalistic, finger-pointing Jesus I grew up with.

Brother Gary was a lot of fun. *That* was different. He was a pastor, but he laughed and cracked jokes. Huh? Are pastors allowed to do that? Also, he acted like he wanted to know me, a mere teenager. He scheduled Sunday night S.N.A.C. for us teens, "Sunday Night After Church." Clever, right? Where were these held? You guessed it: in homes. In that setting he would lead us to make homemade pizza, play games, and have fun. He even had fun when he pulled out a Bible to talk about things that he had learned from it recently. I wondered; what Bible is he using? It sure wasn't like my boring Bible—my childhood Bible that at least had pictures in it. His had no pictures but lots of handwritten notes. That wasn't allowed, not at my house. I wrote in my Bible when I was six years old and got a spanking for it. But his Bible had notes in almost every margin with verses underlined everywhere.

Then he visited my house. *My* house. When I saw him pull into my driveway, I assumed he wanted to see my parents. I called out to him through the screen door, "Hey, Brother Gary, I'll get my mom!" He said, "Hey, is that Roger? I came to see you!"

That scared me to death. Why did he come to see *me*? What (which) sin had he heard I had committed? Maybe he had come to witness to me about salvation. I hurried him downstairs to my basement room before he could reveal my sins in front of my mom. Brother Gary looked over my trophies, posters on the wall, etc. He joked around and we laughed a lot. Then he left. No lecture. No accusations of bad behavior.

Later, my mom asked, "What did the pastor want?" "I dunno." OK, that time my stock teenage answer was actually true. I didn't know what he wanted. But I surmised that he must really be hard up for friends. I decided to return the favor; I went to his house. Again and again.

I usually showed up at night. Maybe even at dinnertime. Go figure. At first, his wife would open the door for me. "Come on in. Gary's in the kitchen." Later, they didn't even bother to open the door for me, just "It's open!" He and I would sit at his dining room table and talk. Well, okay, at times I did most of the talking. I had questions. Lots of questions, but important ones, like, "Why don't girls like me?" He would give some pretty lame answers to questions about my many romantic interests. Stuff like, "Maybe deodorant could help?" Huh? What's that got to do with anything? Those girls didn't need deodorant, so far as I could tell, at least if I could get close enough to any of them to even notice.

Preachers! What do they know about love?

But on most other subjects, Brother Gary was spot on. During those talks at the dining room table, I had a habit of playing with the tiny spoon in his sugar bowl, stirring around the sugar in it while I talked to the sugar bowl, er, to Gary.

When I got married a few years later (miracles do happen!), Brother Gary officiated. He gave me a nicely wrapped gift. Inside was that sugar bowl. It is one of the most precious things I own.

Trust me, your young charges will want to check out your house. As I've said often, you can say and be anything at church for an hour. But they want to know how you live—really live.

Frankly, you will need to decide early that you do not plan to present a "perfect front" to your disciple students. Rather, you will best serve them as a fellow Jesus follower, fumbling at times, but always depending on Jesus to pick you up, dust you off, and keep you moving forward.

START SYSTEMATICALLY:
EMULATE THE BIBLICAL PATTERN

Hopefully, now you are ready to start tackling the "how" of discipling students to grow in their three essential relationships. These relationships will be the focus as we plunge into the rest of this book. The next section, Part Three, is about Equipping your students to relate to God by developing self-disciplined character, or as the Apostle John put it in 1 John 2:14, to become "*strong.*" They will also need to develop Scriptural confidence, as John states, "*and the word abides in you.*" These two components concern their relationship with God (Equipping).

Part Four on Evangelism and Part Five on Encouraging are more about our relationships with people as your disciples learn to engage in God's epic rescue mission and overcome the evil one. Our goal is to help disciples "*overcome the evil one*" (1 John 2:14). To that end, they will be held Accountable for their competency in both their personal mission and ministry with fellow saints.

Combining the three growth components in 1 John 2:12-14 with the three essential relationships in Ephesians 4:11-13 would look something like this:

DISCIPLESHIP RELATIONSHIPS AND GROWTH COMPONENTS

		(Relationship with God)	*(Relationships with People)*	
RELATIONSHIP AREAS (Ephesians 4:11-13)		**EQUIPPING**	**EVANGELIZING**	**ENCOURAGING**
		Relationship with the Lord	Relationships with the Lost	Relationships with the Loved
		(Spiritual Power)	(Spiritual Fruit)	(Spiritual Gifts)
		"equip the saints"	"do works of service"	"edify the body"
ACCOUNTABILITY COMPONENTS (1 John 2:12-14)		1.Self-Disciplined Character	**3. Servant Competencies**	
		"You are strong"		
		2. Scriptural Confidence	*"and you are overcoming the evil one"*	
		"The Word abides in you"		

Now, it's time to begin to flesh out those three essential relationships, which we call Equipping (relating to God), Evangelizing (relating to the lost), and Encouraging (relating to fellow believers). As you can see, we have capitalized those three relationships throughout this book to bring constant attention to them. The rest of this book will address these three all-important disciple relationships through the lens of discipleship with young believers.

PART THREE

STUDENTS OF THE SPIRIT

How to Develop Accountability Level Equipping

CHAPTER 7

YOUR DISCIPLES' PERSONAL GUIDE (AND IT'S NOT YOU)

The WHO of Discipleship: Learning to Rely on the Spirit's Leadership

We all know the Great Commandment: *"Love the Lord your God with all your heart and with all your soul and with all your mind and with all your strength"* (Mark 12:30). But how is this love relationship developed? How do we help our students to connect with God? Who will be their guide? The chapter subhead says it all: it's not you. Your students already have a guide, God's Holy Spirit who lives inside us, the life-giving presence of Jesus.

Of course, I am grateful for my pastor Brother Gary who was there to help me to get my bearings, stay on target, and keep at it, even when I was discouraged or wanted to give up on myself. He was my discipler before I knew what discipleship was really about. And throughout my journey, I could call Brother Gary at the drop of a hat. He was always there for me as a mentor, even long into my journey in youth ministry. I was grateful for him! He had to bear with me a lot in the early days. In fact, it was often a pity party when we talked by phone. "Brother Gary, I'm beating my head against the wall here with my youth group. These teens are giving me fits." He would listen so very patiently. And then, almost without missing a beat, I would hear these words from him: "Well, Roger, I was having my quiet time this morning and read a passage that may be helpful." Then he would refer to a passage, a verse or two from the more than 31,000 verses in the Bible. Yet, that passage spoke directly and clearly to my current problem. I wondered to myself, "How does he *do* that?!" How could he have just that morning read the one verse that would speak to my distinct problem at the exact moment I needed it?

John 14:26 provides insight: "*But the Helper, the Holy Spirit, whom the Father will send in my name, he will teach you all things and bring to your remembrance all that I have said to you.*" Although Brother Gary could not be my constant and ever-present guide, he could point me to his guide, the Holy Spirit. The same Spirit who prompted him to read the Scripture he shared with me during those phone calls. In John 20:22, Jesus "*breathed on them* (the disciples), *and said to them,* '*Receive the Holy Spirit.*'" Brother Gary could not be my constant companion, but the Spirit could! But by constant prayer, I could gain access to God at any moment of any day!

In Greek, "pneuma" refers to spiritual breath. Brother Gary "breathed" spiritually every moment, not just on Sundays. Galatians 5:25 says, "*If we live by the Spirit, let us also keep in step with the Spirit.*" Breathing. Walking. Do you see it? It's a moment-by-moment thing as we breathe in the Living Word and then breathe out His life-giving Word to those around us. Just by living his own life one spiritual breath at a time, Gary was teaching me to do the same as he constantly followed the Spirit. Oh, I was a very slow learner, as I'm sure he would testify. But I did—eventually—

begin to get it. And I do attempt to practice obedient submission to the Spirit daily. I admit, living up to my pastor's example seems like a stretch for me, even now.

DISCIPLES DISCERN THE SPIRIT'S VOICE

Disciples—and disciplers—must discern the Spirit's voice. The very presence of Jesus, by His Spirit, is the ultimate source of help for any of us. He is our breath who gives us life. Without Him, we are without hope. Let us not suppose that Bible lessons alone will produce effective servants of the Lord, but rather Jesus Himself, alive in us. We don't accomplish anything for Jesus; we must learn to let Him do what He alone can do through us. In fact, Jesus told the disciples in John 15:5, "*I am the vine, you are the branches. He who abides in Me, and I in him, bears much fruit; for without Me you can do nothing.*" This is what we pass on to our disciples.

All the Scripture study—even memorization—in the world will not replace the guidance and sweet communion that is available through the Holy Spirit. In fact, He is the one who helps us to understand—and follow—Scripture! Scripture study alone will not suffice. After all, didn't Jesus say that it is the Spirit, the ultimate Equipper, who guides us into the Truth (John 16:13)?

In Romans 8:26, Paul reminds us that the Spirit intercedes for us in our prayers when we don't even know what to pray. The Spirit is at work not only through our Bible reading but also through our prayers! In 1 Thessalonians 3:17, Paul wrote that we should "*pray without ceasing.*" Hmmm, maybe there is something to this? He is our constant guide. 1 Corinthians 2:9-10 reminds us that even though our physical eyes do not see God's future plans for us, "*God has revealed them to us through His Spirit.*" Jude 20–21 reminds us, "*But you, beloved, building yourselves up in your most holy faith and praying in the Holy Spirit, keep yourselves in the love of God, waiting for the mercy of our Lord Jesus Christ that leads to eternal life.*" This chapter is really about prayer, that is, our constant communication with God by His Spirit.

In *The Disciple Maker's Handbook*, Bob Harrington and Josh Patrick wrote, "Disciples cannot be made through fleshly efforts. Jesus, in His humanity, fully acknowledged His dependence upon the Spirit. Disciple making is not just a good strategy . . . it is a way of life, accomplished through the fruit of the Holy Spirit living through a person's yielded and holy life (2 Corinthians 3:16–17). If Jesus fully depended on the Holy Spirit's power, how can we do any less?"[9]

What then are we to teach young disciples? How to read the Bible? How to study? How to witness? How to serve in the Church? We-l-l, yes. But does discipleship really come down to what we can know about Jesus academically or achieve for Jesus? No, you don't believe that. When discipleship is said and done, it is about submitting to His Lordship in all aspects of life. It's about yielding to His power, learning to trust Him alone for insight, direction, and boldness. All those other things will happen as we obey Him. Your discipling is about teaching, but not merely in an academic sense. Instead, you are teaching disciples to surrender to Jesus as they listen to Him and obey His Spirit's every whispered command. That is exciting stuff!

In fact, is this not what we have been looking for in our young disciples? We have desired that our young protégés would learn Jesus, not merely in an academic sense, but truly know Him and be known by Him, relationally. More importantly, isn't this relationship what Jesus wants?

Jesus' last teaching to His disciples before His arrest was during their final Passover meal together. He told the disciples that He would continue to be present with them and guide them by His Spirit. He explained the Spirit's role in John 16:13: *"But when he, the Spirit of truth, comes, he will guide you into all the truth. He will not speak on his own; he will speak only what he hears, and he will tell you what is yet to come."* Guide us into truth? Tell us things yet to come? Are you kidding me? Who wouldn't want a personal guide like that? We welcome insight into what is yet to come. It is accessible. He is accessible. He is right there, residing within every believer, waiting to guide each of us individually. We learn as we commune with Him in prayer.

Where Do We Begin?

I remember the morning after I first came to Jesus as a teenager. When I awoke that morning, my very first thought was that Jesus had truly come into my life the night before! I was awestruck. But immediately after that, I panicked. I quickly realized, "I don't know how to do this! I don't know how to follow Jesus. I know church. I know how to do religion, even Christianity. But I haven't got a clue what to do when it comes to listening to Jesus and doing what He says. I'm not even sure I will be able to recognize His voice when He speaks!"

I was forlorn. But only for one brief moment. Then it occurred to me: Jesus knew exactly what He got when He got me. Basically, an ignoramus. Yet, somehow, deep in my own spirit the very night before, I had heard Jesus speak to me loud and clear. I thought, "If Jesus wants to speak to little ole' me, He did it once already, so I'm sure He will find a way to get my attention." Meanwhile, I just started asking Him a bunch of questions in my prayers, like:

- "What should I wear today, Jesus?"
- "Where would You like me to sit in the cafeteria during lunch, Jesus?"
- "Jesus, are you asking me to talk to that guy at his locker now, for real?"

I'll admit, I didn't carry on this new internal conversation with Jesus' Spirit perfectly or even consistently. But I did do it a lot. I pestered Jesus with questions. I was like a child, full of all kinds of mostly silly questions for his parents.

Thankfully, Brother Gary was also close by to help. The Spirit worked through his godly advice to affirm God's directives. Discipler, as you dive into spiritual disciplines with your young disciples, pointing them to the Spirit of Jesus should be one of your highest priorities. After all, you are temporary; the Spirit is available 24/7 to all believers who seek Him in constant prayer.

Like Jesus, we must be keenly attentive to God's will. How so? Ephesians 5:17–18 is one of those verses where God declares clearly and succinctly His will for us. He said, "*Therefore, do not be foolish, but understand what the Lord's will is. Do not get drunk on wine . . . but instead be filled with the Spirit.*" Wait, God's will is to not get drunk on wine? Yes, but God is really just emphasizing that we are controlled by what fills us. He wants us to be controlled by the Spirit. We are to be filled by the Spirit who resides within us and quietly speaks God's will to us. He is there, not as a maid to clean up our messes or a mascot to cheer on our own decisions, but as the Master who guides our every step. In John 10:3, Jesus tells us that "*the sheep listen to his voice.*" Verse 4 says that "*they follow him because they know his voice.*" What a privilege it is to help our disciples recognize the Spirit's voice when He calls them by name!

What does God's voice sound like? Well, we know two things, at least. His voice is:

- Unique. He speaks uniquely according to the person and the circumstance. He spoke to Job in the whirlwind in Job 40:6. But when God spoke to Elijah in 1 Kings 19:12, He didn't speak in a whirlwind but in a still, small voice. The Holy Spirit resides inside; His voice is as close as our own breath. He speaks to each believer personally and uniquely.
- Unchanging: The Spirit's voice is not only unique but also unchanging, aligning consistently with Scripture. Be certain of this: His instruction will sound just like God's written Word. The Spirit will not contradict the Scriptures.

We learn to discern His voice as we read and study His Word to become all He intended!

DISCIPLES DISPEL SPIRITUAL DULLNESS

We easily recognize the voices of those in our lives with whom we spend time. I can still hear my Grandma Reed's voice in my mind to this day, decades after I spent time with her as a child. Why do we not recognize the Spirit's voice when He is closer to us than our own breath?

The problem is, our young disciples have a considerable amount of noise pollution filling their minds from cell phones, media, movies, friends, and, yes, the evil one. These all tend to dull their hearing and drown out the Spirit's voice. Many young people have opened their minds to the world instead of the Spirit. This only allows the Devil's fiery darts to invade their thoughts, inflame their passions, and block their communion with God (Ephesians 6:16).

Have you ever sensed that you were being spoken to, but nobody was around? And worse, the words you were hearing in your mind seemed, well, kind of counterintuitive? Like a prompting to turn right instead of turning left along your usual drive home? Or like, "Go over there and talk to that complete stranger!?"

I confess, I have often reacted to these spontaneous inner prompts with, "Huh, wh-a-a? Where did that idea come from? Wow, that thought was weird. I'm certainly not going to do that!" In that moment, I simply had not recognized the Spirit's voice. Once, while speaking at a school assembly, I had hoped to offer students a chance to respond publicly. They sat like stones as I spoke. At the last second, I chickened out. I said, "Our worship team is going to sing. After that, we will be dismissed; if you want to talk to us, please feel free." But as the team sang, I heard the Spirit say, "You are really going to deny these students a chance to respond? I have students ready to follow Me! Get back up there and give them a chance." Sheepishly, I stood and told the students that we were going to allow them to respond publicly to Christ. A few moments passed. No movement: yep, just as I had suspected. Then one young lady at the very top bleacher stood up and began to make her way to the gym floor. I thought, "Well, Father, I guess one is willing." Then, to my amazement, students began to rise and walk down to join her. I had to go up into the stands, which had almost emptied, to address the hundreds who came to the gym floor to publicly respond to Christ. I'll never forget that moment. Exhilarating, but also humbling.

Ephesians 4:30 urges us to "*not grieve the Holy Spirit of God, by whom you were sealed for the day of redemption.*" And 1 Thessalonians 5:19

warns us not to *"quench the Spirit."* I wonder how many amazing moments I have missed because I did not recognize and obey the voice of the Holy Spirit who was prompting me toward a small miracle. I shudder to think.

That voice has come to me often, every day. Dull instrument that I am, I have sadly missed opportunities at times because I was preoccupied with other concerns, other voices. I am still learning to listen. Nevertheless, I really want to help young disciples hear His voice!

When they—we—experience no miracles, we can easily stop believing in them, oh, except of course, in theory. You know, God spoke to people in the Bible, but that is pretty distant from our daily drudgery. That stuff only happens in the Bible, right? Wrong. But we fail to listen!

I was with Daniel, one of our Global Institute interns, on the way to speak at a church in South Georgia one Sunday morning. I had been assigned to cover a specific Scripture passage in a sermon series. This one was about the Spirit's leadership and sacrificing good for best. Oh, my. I was really concerned about how these subjects would be received.

We departed at 5:00am, so by the time we reached our destination, I could tell my guy was hungry. Growing boy, you know. Or was that my stomach growling? I started looking for a donut shop to stop into and grab a donut and some coffee. We saw no donut shops, but then I sensed an inner prompting to stop at a grocery store. There was no indication that we would find a bakery there. Fortunately, there was a small bakery with a seating area. We grabbed coffee and donuts and sat at a table to shove them down before heading to the church.

While we were munching, a young man crossed behind me. Out of the blue, he said, "Good morning, gentlemen." Huh? Who is this? Did he not know that these days we charge forward on our way to wherever, barely looking up to see anyone in our path? This was not only a guy (men don't speak to men they don't know without a reason, not even to ask for directions). This was also a *young* man. Those types are often lost in their cell phones as they walk. But this stranger greeted us on his way to wherever. Unusual!

I had an impression: "If that guy comes back this way, talk to him." That sounded a little nervy. But perhaps this was the Spirit, right? "I'll do it, Lord, if You pass him by our way again!"

And then, here he came, walking in our direction. I waved him over. "Who are you, young man?" He smiled. "My name is Dylan." "Well, Dylan," I said, "you are different." He said, "I know." I asked him why he greeted us, total strangers. To my surprise, he said, "Well, the Spirit told me to say hi. That happens often; I'm just minding my business and the Spirit prompts me to do weird stuff. But it's actually kind of cool." Huh? Here was a young guy talking to perfect strangers about the Lord, even bringing up the Holy Spirit!

I asked him if he went to church. He mentioned the name of a Baptist church he attended. (I'm thinking, what kind of Baptist church talks about Holy Spirit stuff? And don't get mad because I jumped on the Baptists; I *am* a Baptist.) He then proceeded to tell me that he had spent three years in prison, that he had been involved with drugs and alcohol and got into some big trouble. After landing in prison, he met Jesus, who totally changed his life.

Later in our brief conversation, Dylan had another surprise. He said, "I have a word from the Lord for you today. Do you want to hear it?" Did I ever! He said, "The word is 'sacrifice.' We need to be willing to sacrifice lesser things to follow Jesus." With that, he said his goodbyes, and we were left sitting there, kind of in awe of what happened. I turned to my young friend Daniel and said, "Did you hear what that guy just said? He must have been reading my sermon outline! He hit a huge point in my message today with just a couple of sentences!"

Both of us sat absorbing it for just a minute. I could visualize a slight smirk on the Holy Spirit's face as He gently whispered, "See there, let this be a reminder that if you just keep hanging with Me, I will show you where to get donuts . . . and confirm your message topic through perfect strangers. I'm also helping your young protégé beside you to listen to me better! Get it?"

Just three weeks later, Daniel returned from Christmas break. He told me of moments when he sensed the Spirit prompting him to go out of his way to reach out to strangers—even to a homeless woman at a gas station. Those moments had produced crazy adventures. He even witnessed to a school friend of his who had professed to be an atheist . . . and led him to faith in Christ. Get it? Oh, yes, Lord, I got it.

I believe the Spirit wants to make life an adventure. He wants to give us little "atta boys," small victories along the way each day, even as we look to Him for the best location to grab donuts. And when we don't? Well, chalk up another one for the Devil who wants to distract us from that still, small voice and ultimately convince us that we are basically on our own to live the life we were called to experience. Satan's plan is distraction, drudgery, and defeat. Your precious young disciples desperately need to recognize his deception. They need to listen to the Spirit's voice in the smallest incidents to prepare the way for greater miracles, even moving mountains.

As we listen and obey, those little victories stack up. They fuel greater faith in God's power. They inspire bigger risks in the days to come. They incentivize us to move toward even greater future victories. But it seems that we are far too prone to get lost in day-to-day concerns, our cell phones, and other distractions. Then, distracted from His voice, we miss the adventure.

What am I saying here? I am saying that one of the most important things you can do with your disciples is to follow the Holy Spirit on a moment-by-moment basis and then lead them to do the same! D.L. Moody once said, "You might as well try to see without eyes, hear without ears, or breathe without lungs, as to try to live the Christian life without the Holy Spirit."[10] Got it?

I can hear you say it. "Hey, Roger, is there a manual for that to teach to my disciples?" Well, yes; it's called the Bible. The more believers ingest that book, the more they will become acquainted with the still, small voice of the Holy Spirit. The more we feed on its Truth, the more power we will have to walk in the Spirit. The more easily we will "breathe" by His life-giving Spirit.

The goal of discipleship, at its core, is pretty simple: learning to follow Jesus by hearing and obeying His Spirit every moment. That path will never lead to a dull life, no way! With that in mind, let's consider the very distinct responsibilities involved in discipling young disciples. Hopefully, with hearts attentive to the Spirit, we are ready to proceed from the "Who" to the "what" and the "how" of discipling. The question before us in the next chapter is, "What is the essence of discipling, and how do we focus our young disciples upon the initial task of developing the character of Christ through self-discipline?"

CHAPTER 8

DESIRING SELF-DISCIPLINE

The WHAT of Discipleship: Learning Self-Discipline

The initial step for following Jesus is learning to listen to His Spirit. But the other part is consistently obeying His voice. Disciples must choose obedience. It is a voluntary response to God's love and cannot be forced. There is a strategic blend between your relationship with young disciples as a discipler and their own personal initiative to relate to Jesus. You can persuade them and even exert considerable influence. But you can't make them grow. And you can't do the students' work for them. It requires a genuine desire to be fruitful. Accountability is the middle stage of believers' growth, and it has three components that are unique to it. Let's explore!

DISCIPLESHIP IS BASED ON THREE GROWTH COMPONENTS

We all know that learning is more caught than taught. As the disciples followed Jesus everywhere, they learned. A lot. They learned who God is. They learned how we relate to God even in the routine of daily life. They learned from Jesus how to properly respond to events that swirled around them as they followed the Master. Certainly, they learned more than just spiritual stuff. They learned life; you know, mundane things like:

- How to handle money. Remember that annoying mountain lesson in Matthew 6:19–21 about not storing up treasures on earth?
- How to treat one another. There was that awkward moment when James and John's mother asked Jesus to place them over the other disciples in the pecking order (Matthew 20).
- Oh, yikes; there was also that awful injunction to love our enemies (Matthew 5:44).
- How to value little children, honor the poor, bless outcasts, and so much more.

Discipleship is about life, not just about intellectual knowledge, or religious behaviors. Shocker, right? As we noted in the first chapter, the Apostle John specifies three identifying components of a true spiritual "youth." Based on 1 John 2:12-14, the Global Institute addresses these three basic Accountability components to help our interns grow in all three essential relationships:

- Spiritual Character (heart): discipleship begins with voluntary self-discipline to become like Jesus.
- Scriptural Confidence (head): we teach Bible content and study skills to provide a solid foundation.
- Servant Leader Competencies (hands): we train for effective service, not just head knowledge.

These three are like three strands of a rope; each strand is essential to its strength. The first two components concern our relationship with God; we will address both here in Part Three. Later, in Parts

Four and Five, we will address the final component, which is about relating to people. But discipleship begins here, as disciples form the character of Jesus. Paul identified this process as being conformed to the image of Christ. Disciplers need to learn how Jesus influenced His disciples to eagerly embrace self-discipline, growing just as He did in all areas of life.

DISCIPLESHIP BEGINS WITH THE CHARACTER OF CHRIST (HEART)

The importance of the first aspect—the character-building phase of your disciples' development—cannot be overestimated. Someone once observed, regarding securing a job, that knowledge or skill may get you in the door of employment, but your character will keep you there. So true. Don't make the mistake of thinking that discipling your students consists only of imparting great Bible knowledge, perhaps with the addition of a few spiritual skillsets.

No, no, no. We start with their character. All aspects of it! Disciples must acquire healthy life habits, growing just as Jesus did to become like Him. Luke 2:52 tells us that Jesus grew in wisdom (intellectual growth), and in stature (physical growth), and in favor with God (spiritual growth) and man (social growth). These four disciplines are foundational to serving others effectively. In fact, at the Global Institute, we call these four disciplines the "Four Pillars" because our future effectiveness rests upon our character. This reminds us that the process of discipling definitely cannot be confined to an hour-long Bible study. It involves your disciples' daily individual investment in all aspects of their lives . . . even when you are not around.

You know there are limits to the amount of time you can spend with your disciples. Your goal is to help them embrace for themselves the value of shaping the character of Christ in their own personal relationship with Him. For these young people, it will be a matter of the heart.

What they may not initially understand is that building any relationship requires discipline, mostly self-discipline. Of course, holding students Accountable is a strategic part of discipleship. During the discipleship process, we will ask probing questions, like:

- What are you reading from the Word this week?
- How have you lived out the things you are learning from Christ lately?
- What temptations have you been dealing with this week?
- How has your influence grown among lost acquaintances, friends, or family?
- What can we be praying with you in the coming week?

Even so, we must bear in mind that students cannot truly be held accountable unless there is a real desire to grow, which involves self-discipline. 2 Timothy 1:7 places self-discipline in a strategic role; "*For the Spirit God gave us does not make us timid, but gives us power, love and self-discipline.*" What are we to learn from this passage which contains a triad of valuable traits?

Power? We know that God's power embodies His strength, authority, law, and justice. God could not ignore man's sin. Justice demanded a penalty. Deep within us there is a cry for justice. This is the character of God which He has also built into humankind. And what about love? God also imparts a spirit of love. Thus, His mercy, grace and forgiveness fit into the equation, too!

The divine tension is evident here. What holds these two opposites—law and love—in balance? Only one thing could satisfy God's just law while exhibiting His love at the same time. Law and love were held together by Jesus' self-discipline as He willingly endured the Cross. Yes, self-discipline is to be prized. If disciples are to overcome, they will need both law and love, but these qualities must be held in a precarious and delicate balance. Law that runs amuck will be haughty, even deadly. Love unchecked will ignore justice, which is unthinkable.

Self-discipline is God's answer to the dilemma. His law demanded justice. His love put Him on a cross to satisfy that demand. It was His self-discipline that kept Him there, and that is why we love Him so. He did not call ten thousand angels to rescue Him. When we could neither escape God's law nor earn His love, Jesus' amazing self-discipline satisfied both. We gladly discipline ourselves for Him because we love Him. Ultimately, that is what obedience looks like. And that is why we voluntarily choose self-discipline. Character transformation through self-discipline is a response to God's merciful salvation, not a means to achieve it.

Character has to do with relationships, beginning with God and extending to other people. Jim Wilder wrote in Rare Leadership, "Character is our spontaneous embedded responses to our relational environment, behavior that is automatic and flows from the heart."[11] Embedded? Automatic? Self-discipline builds habits that display the character of Christ to a waiting world.

DISCIPLESHIP BUILDS CHARACTER THROUGH SELF-DISCIPLINE

Gaining the character of Christ is a 24/7 discipline; that means that you will not be able to be present with your young disciples for most of it. This will be about their personal initiative in their home, at school, or at work, apart from meetings where you are with them in person. They must truly desire to be more like their Master, Jesus.

How do we influence such change? This will take time. Before we can discuss the content of discipleship, we must get the context right. Creating a foundation for growth involves more than passing along a few spiritual disciplines. It is about leading our disciples to live every part of their lives in loving relationship with God and man. How do we help them truly desire it?

Shouldn't discipleship begin with Bible study? We-l-l, that would be accurate. Sort of. But hold on! Remember the first two disciples in John 1? Jesus turned and confronted them as they followed Him (oops, awkward!) and asked, "What do you want?" Their reply? Those impertinent kids asked, "Where are you staying?" What a bare-faced, back door self-invitation!

But notice Jesus' response. He was on to their game. He said, "Come and see." Next thing we know, John and Andrew are hanging with Jesus and, you know, probably eating His food, too! Formal teaching? Hardly. Jesus' "come and see" was a wide-open invitation. This was an invitation for those young guys—and us— to study Jesus up close and personal. We only have to look at what Jesus did with the first disciples to discover how to teach our own young disciples.

But wait! Before we dive into the four self-disciplines of a Christlike character, I know you may be wondering why we don't concentrate only on the spiritual aspects. You might even be protesting that the other personal self-disciplines should be instilled by the teens' parents. And you would be right. Actually, all four of them. But I have breaking news: Our culture is dissuading students from either submitting to authority *or* accepting personal responsibility. We can no longer assume that our disciples already get this; rather, we may need to recognize that they may *not* get the need for either submission or self-discipline. Even parents who have faithfully imparted these values to their teens will welcome your support. While you may not be able to assume full responsibility to train students in every aspect of self-discipline, you will need to at least address all of them openly and honestly.

So, there it is. Discipleship is about discipline in all areas of life, not just spiritual disciplines. It is about learning to take care of one's own growth rather than assuming that others will take care of it. To ignore the imperative of self-discipline is to build upon a foundation of sand.

Remember: It is not about you disciplining them, as in carrying around a big stick. No, in the end it must be about their own desire to discipline themselves to follow Jesus in every aspect of their lives. The objective for character development is self-discipline! Perhaps we should explore these disciplines in a little more detail.

Disciples Should Grow in Integrity Through Intellectual Self-Disciplines

First, Luke 2:52 explains that Jesus grew in wisdom. Wisdom is not just about factual knowledge. It's about both biblical learning and applying biblical truth to daily living. Our integrity is based upon a cohesive and consistent adherence to truth in all aspects of our lives. As Proverbs 1:7 reminds us, "*The fear of the Lord is the beginning of knowledge, but fools despise wisdom and instruction.*" The authority of God's Word matters. Sadly, many of our teens live in a culture that has traded facts for fables. Facts can be so inconvenient.

Intellectually, young disciples must bring everything under God's authority, even applying wisdom to values like financial stewardship and time management. When teenagers have most necessities taken care of, they may become preoccupied with peripheral matters. If food appears on the table daily without fail and without any effort or expense on their part, teens can turn up their noses at good food without a second thought. You get the picture. The more we indulge teens, the more likely it is that they will take basic necessities like food, clothing, and shelter for granted. They may then pursue self-indulgent pleasures because they are unaffected and thus, unconcerned with such realities. The likely result? Ingratitude, entitlement, superiority, or worse. Proper work ethic becomes a casualty of an entitled mentality.

When teens are not grounded in factual reality, both they and people around them are negatively affected. They need both the facts and the capacity to skillfully apply facts to the challenges of daily living. Wisdom is the capacity to apply the facts both to immediate situations and to the wider context of timeless truth that enables us to live well and at peace with God and man. Wisdom will assess immediate needs, but also take a 30,000-foot view to consider how immediate solutions may affect other relationships, as well as similar future situations that we will face with our families, friends, and the culture.

Wisdom and morality go hand in hand. When society ignores the moral underpinnings that enable it to run properly, it will eventually experience a collective cultural free fall. Personal integrity goes out the window. Young people will then grow up in a chaotic environment where there are few, if any, boundaries on their behavior; instead, immediate gratification is the goal.

It is partly because of this lack of guardrails that many school systems stepped in to assume a parenting role. They are teaching sex education in the place of parents and moral values in the place of the Church. Things have changed.

And what does discipleship have to do with this dilemma? For starters, we will need to help our disciples acquire critical thinking skills. As it stands today, many teens believe they can get all the information they need from social media. They assume that they need only access—but not assess—that information. This leaves them prey to the dark side of media indoctrination, guided by feelings rather than by facts. Tim Elmore observed, "They don't need us for information. They need us for interpretation."[12] Teens need the Word, not just the web.

Beyond that, guardrails are even coming down in many school systems as they have moved away from enforcing boundaries. One high school counselor in the Atlanta area related to me that their incoming school board implemented a ban on most disciplinary actions. Instead, the students were to be treated with kid gloves and counseled to seek deeper reasons for their bad behavior. Which becomes a blame game (victimhood). She said, "Once the students realized that this was happening, it was like the inmates took over the asylum." The downward slide into chaos was swift and overwhelming for everyone. Administrators knew that the new policies would not work. But the new school board seemed to have no interest in disciplining misbehaving students.

Boundaries seem to be a thing of the past. But Psalm 16:5–6 says, "*Lord, you alone are my portion and my cup; you make my lot secure. The boundary lines have fallen for me in pleasant places.*" His boundary lines are designed to enable us to live well, not to restrict us. Disciples learn to respect boundaries and boundary keepers.

They recognize and respond to their authorities' position, not their personality. But they judge all by the Word, the final authority.

Discipleship should help your students to become solutions-oriented in a variety of settings, just as young Joseph in Genesis did when he dealt with the Egyptians. This will involve asking questions, posing problems to be solved, and leading them to seek biblical guidance for the situations they face both now and in the future. And it will mean holding disciples accountable for their decision-making. They must learn to do right even when it doesn't feel good. They even recognize that not all pain is bad; persevering is often what produces good results.

To this end, disciples know that merely downloading facts is insufficient. Discipleship is not about transferring facts from Bibles to brains. Reading the Bible in a daily quiet time is good but not enough. They will need help to carefully study Scripture on a regular basis with the goal of understanding life as the Creator intended it to be lived. Our objective is not merely that they listen to our teaching, important as that may be. Instead, we want to enable them to search out the Truth of God's Word for themselves, guided by the Spirit, even when we are not present.

We want them to ask questions about what they read and probe deeper to glean the rich truths of Scripture. In 2 Timothy 3:15, Paul reminded young Timothy that *"from infancy you have known the Holy Scriptures which are able to make you wise for salvation through faith in Christ Jesus."* The end goal for the disciples is not knowledge only, but wisdom that leads to good works! Verses 16–17 read, *"All Scripture is God-breathed and is useful for teaching, rebuking, correcting and training in righteousness, so that the servant of God may be thoroughly equipped for every good work."*

Disciples Must Develop Initiative in Physical Self-Disciplines

Jesus grew physically. Does attention to physical growth seem far-fetched from discipleship? I mean, really? Are we saying that as disciplers of teenagers, we need to be concerned about their physical discipline? Uh, yes. They must exhibit initiative in their own self-care before they can earn the right to engage others to embrace self-discipline. 1 Corinthians 3:16 reminds us that our bodies are the temple of God's Holy Spirit. God must replace our heart of stone; it is deceitfully wicked. He must transform our minds (Romans 12:1-2). What then is left? He wants us to make our bodies His temple, a living sacrifice. Taking care of our temple is clearly a discipleship goal.

Ask yourself, "Do my student disciples attend to their physical health, like watching what and how much they eat? Or what medications or drugs they ingest? Do they take care of their personal hygiene and appearance? Do they use these things to draw attention to themselves, or do they seek their physical well-being as a means to glorify their Heavenly Father?" Since 2 Corinthians 5:20 tells us that we are ambassadors for Christ, shouldn't this matter?

And that's just the beginning. Do they take the initiative to make their own bed and keep their room clean, or do they have to be nagged? Do they expect others to follow after them and clean up the messes they leave behind? Do they throw away their trash at the fast-food place or walk away and let the paid help take care of that for them? When leaving an empty room, do they turn off the lights? These habits help disciples develop character . . . and credibility.

In the midst of all the environmental uproar, let me gently point out that we were all called to be stewards of our planet by God Himself. Genesis 1:28 tells us to subdue and rule the earth. Some young people may be focused on saving the earth's environment, but do they recognize that they must begin by keeping their own bedroom clean, helping with household chores, and reining in consumerist appetites? These are things young disciples can do now! It's about being responsible, taking the initiative to do their part, all in a spirit of servanthood.

When possible, visit your disciples' homes. Check out their room. If their room is a pigsty, you may rightly wonder whether their spiritual space is likewise unkempt and undisciplined.

Yes, there's even more. What about their sexuality? I can hear you ranting in my ear now: "Oh, no, sir! Sex does not appear on any list of discipleship topics I've ever seen!" Okay, maybe. But it should have been there, especially when discipling teenagers who are grappling with their sexuality! Learning to restrain their sexual urges provides at least one solid evidence that they are holding themselves accountable to control their own behavior.

This will likely not be easy. Discipline in sexuality is the exact opposite of what is being broadcast loudly in our world today. Not only is the culture telling teens they should freely obey their sexual urges, but they are also now being told that they can greatly expand their gender options to suit themselves. Kind of like a sexual smorgasbord.

Genesis 1:27 says, "*So God created mankind in his own image, in the image of God he created them; male and female he created them.*" But today, having only two options seems far too limiting. Who is God to tell us who we are to be? It's like we are shaking our fist in His face and saying, "God, you will not tell me who I am or limit me in any way, especially with this first decision You made (and without my permission) to determine my gender at my conception."

We want to be sensitive as we address this, but neither nature nor science will accede to this rebellion. Gender is determined at the millisecond of conception. It is permanently sealed in our DNA. Neither your disciples nor their friends get to choose. Your disciples need to grasp that it was God who fearfully and wonderfully made them to fulfill His strategic purpose for every person in His Kingdom. To pursue sexual independence from God's design is not only harmful to individuals, but it also introduces confusion and chaos into the community at large. So, yes, physical discipline—every part of it—is vital to our youths' discipleship, now more than ever.

Disciples Must Gain Influence by Social Self-Disciplines

We were created by a triune God to be relational. As God relates perfectly within the Trinity, He also created humanity to be relational with Him and with one another. How will our disciples carry out the Great Commission if they have poor or even unhealthy relationships with others, beginning at home but extending into all other spheres? The Covid pandemic negatively impacted teens' social skills even more. Their social presence affects their influence for Christ.

Selflessness should be a mark of a young disciple. Jesus advocated that believers go the second mile in serving others, beyond what is required. If your young disciples' relationships with their parents or siblings at home are strained (in the first and foremost laboratory of social learning skills), how can we assume that they will have healthy social skills at school, their workplace, or later, in their own marriage? Since discipleship involves Evangelism, can we ignore a disciple's unhealthy interactions with others? If they cannot get along with their own family or fellow believers at home and church, how will they influence godless schoolmates or a messed-up boss or crazy relatives on a wider platform?

Our disciples will need to take the initiative to carry their own weight. They do not make their peers do their work for them or supervisors do their thinking for them.

Even etiquette and manners are social skills that help us to restrain ourselves so other people are not burdened by our otherwise slovenly ways. In light of the Great Commission, our social interactions with other people matter. This cannot be ignored as we attempt to help young disciples learn self-discipline in all areas of their lives. Monitoring both their speech and actions will impact their influence in sharing the light of Christ with others.

Social media has become a huge focus. The statistics on the amount of time teenagers spend in front of a screen are staggering. What do your disciples look at on screen? How long do they spend on media? What is their social footprint? Their online identity? Their influence for Christ is at stake, even there. In this tech age, these will need to be subjects for honest discussion!

One helpful tool for all areas of self-discipline may be fasting. We often associate this discipline only with the physical area. But perhaps we should also ask our disciples to consider fasting from things other than food. Perhaps they could fast from over-scheduling. Or shopping. They may fast from their cell phones, social media, or the news media. When combined with increased time in prayer and Scripture study, fasting can be a helpful self-discipline tool.

When discipling teenagers, intellectual, physical, and social disciplines must go hand in hand with spiritual disciplines. The discipler's role includes supporting and assisting parents to reinforce young disciples' personal disciplines. While this role may not be your favorite responsibility, it is foundational to your—and your disciple's—success.

Disciples Should Develop Insight in Spiritual Self-Disciplines

Yes, I know that I put spiritual discipline last, out of order. Sorry, but I just wanted to be clear that while spiritual disciplines are of foremost importance, spiritual life cannot and must not be segmented away from other aspects of a disciple's life. This fact is hugely important to consider in any effort to disciple teenagers. Spiritual discipline is first about our disciples' submission to God's authority. Humans are broken by sin and seek freedom from authority, especially God's. Never has this rebellion been more apparent than in today's culture, one that first demanded to be unhindered, and now is becoming unhinged. However, as students grow in their relationship with God, they will seek self-disciplined submission to Him in all things.

Yes, we desire that they develop spiritual disciplines that will continue throughout their lives, like personal prayer and journaling, fasting, and Bible habits such as individual reading and deeper study. And they need instruction through our teaching; we will get to that in the very next chapter. But the thing is, this all begins with their decision to submit their lives to God and then follow Him in their personal efforts to develop spiritual muscle in every area of their lives.

Of all the areas of Jesus' growth that you emphasize with your disciples, the spiritual aspect may be the most challenging. It may be easier to see results in the other disciplines.

You may ask your students to hold each other accountable to read much or all the Bible on a designated schedule, to memorize several verses per week and retain them over time, to develop their prayer life with God, and maybe keep a prayer journal. These habits will be instilled with great exertion, even with your positive influence brought to bear. Trust me, you will be tested in your resolve to hold your students accountable. You will expend relational capital with your disciples to influence them to grow in character through spiritual self-disciplines.

We know that we cannot hold a class for an hour or so each week in the church building to teach Scripture and call it discipleship. Jesus lived with His disciples, and while we cannot do that, we can grow relationships with our students. In that context, we don't just teach them, but we *show* them how to follow Jesus simply because of His great love for them.

Are We Ready Now to Tackle the Second Component?

Merely teaching the Scriptures may have little effect until our young disciples are motivated to Equip themselves with self-disciplines that will reflect Christ's character more consistently. Character development is where we begin as we help students develop self-disciplines that reflect their love for Jesus (heart). This is the pathway to future credibility with other people. Before anything else happens, they must become spiritually strong, as noted in 1 John 2:14.

The remainder of Part Three will deal with our disciples' confidence in Scripture (head), the second of three growth components of discipleship. Character-building is a matter of the heart, as disciples desire to become more like the One they love. But they also deepen their relationship with Jesus by growing their confidence in His Word as He speaks to them through its pages. In the next chapter let's see just how Jesus instilled Scriptural confidence in His disciples.

CHAPTER 9

DISCIPLING LIKE JESUS

The HOW of Equipping:
Instilling Confidence through Scripture

Our relationship with Jesus involves both our heart and our head. The two are not separate, nor is one less important than the other for disciples to be prepared to serve. We are Equipped to become strong as we develop the character of self-discipline that Jesus exemplified. We also develop confidence in Scripture as the Word abides in us, as John described in 1 John 2:12-14.

Content, the "what" of our Faith, is vital for disciples to gain confidence. Our strength is grounded in the Word. John identified Jesus as the Word (John 1:1). Jesus didn't just know the Word, He IS the Word. Jesus, the Living Word, may be found in Scripture, the Written Word. There we find the Truth that sets us free: "*If you hold to my teaching, you are really my disciples. Then you will know the truth, and the truth will set you free*" (John 8:31–32). Jesus quoted Deuteronomy 8:3 in Matthew 4:4, "*Man shall not live by bread alone, but by every word that proceeds from the mouth of God.*" Jesus knew His disciples needed solid content. He even called

Himself their food (John 6:35, 53-58). How important is food? Well, you can't live without it.

DISCIPLESHIP MUST PURSUE SCRIPTURE-BASED SUBJECTS

So, what is the "what" that we pass on to our young disciples? You probably want a definitive list of topics to discuss with your disciples, right? I thought so. I can give you a starter list of sorts, but probably not an exhaustive list. Why not? Because the needs of your students will differ, depending on how their church and their families have prepared them through teaching, sermons, and other content-rich opportunities that the students have already received.

What follows is a basic list of topics that you should consider. Several, if not all, of these topics may require multiple sessions.

Topics for Equipping Relationship with the Master:

- Basic Bible doctrines (Trinity, Jesus' work, Scripture, eternal security of believers, etc.)
- Training in the four self-disciplines (growing in wisdom, stature, and favor with God and man)
- The person, purpose, and personal guidance of the Spirit
- Praying corporately, individually, continually
- How to study the Bible and pass its truth on to others
- Scripture memory and meditation plans and helps

Topics for Evangelizing Relationships in the Marketplace:

- Producing spiritual fruit
- Basics of personal Evangelism
- Apologetics and critical thinking

- Spiritual warfare

Topics for Encouraging Relationships with Ministry Mates:

- The attitude of servanthood
- Discovering spiritual gifts
- Body life—how to serve in the Church
- Getting along with fallen people (personality testing, conflict resolution, etc.)

There are so many great curriculums to choose from to address all these topics. In addition to the topics above, consider studying through at least one Gospel and the book of Acts together.

Develop a plan that fits your young disciples, and then find a curriculum or studies that will follow that plan. Just remember that delivering content alone will not produce overcomers. They must also learn how to study on their own, and then learn how to help others learn from them.

DISCIPLESHIP SHOULD PRACTICE THE SAVIOR'S TEACHING STYLE

Beyond the "what" of our teaching is the "how" of our teaching. How we help our disciples begin to feed (Equip) themselves is very important! Jesus pointed to Scripture in all things, teaching His disciples both formally and informally. Let's explore Jesus' example and pay close attention to His teaching style. He utilized a variety of approaches. So should we.

Formal Learning

The first thing many people think of when we discuss discipleship is Bible study. The study of core beliefs about our Faith is an essential discipling element. Jesus certainly gave lectures to His disciples concerning the fundamentals, as He did on the Mount (Matthew 5–7). That sermon was primarily focused upon His disciples. Jesus intentionally engaged His disciples to help them acquire biblical insight and wisdom.

But before we describe His teaching methods, let's be fair: The problem with much of what is called discipleship is that the experience is limited pretty much to just that—sit and study.

Imagine that. We know that Jesus taught His disciples. But did His teaching consist of classroom lectures? Hardly. Do you think those brawny fishermen would have been drawn to that sort of experience in discipleship? No. Obviously, Jesus' disciples had a far more robust expectation of their experience with Him than that. They went where He went. They watched what He did. They did what He said. They practiced what He taught while ever on the move with Him.

Then, in the midst of all that, He sat them down and taught them. And when He did, they were ready to listen. Even when Jesus lectured, He often took the disciples outside and sat down on the side of a mountain to teach them. Much of their formal learning took place in a rather informal setting in which Jesus utilized an experiential teaching style.

I recognize that a dining room table setting may be needed for some, if not much, of your teaching times with your students. They will need to study Bible doctrines, discuss theology, take notes, and so on. We must teach them to ask hermeneutical (interpretation) questions about the text, such as who said it, when, to whom, why, and whether the passage is descriptive (for that time only) or prescriptive (to all for all times). But when you do this, break out the sodas and some refreshments! Make even the formal teaching times rich in personalized fellowship with God and with each other that is centered in the Word.

Informal Teachable Moments

Mark 12:41–44 gives us insight into how Jesus also used everyday occurrences to teach His disciples, sort of on-the-fly. On that occasion as He observed several rich men who gave to the Temple treasury, Jesus noted one poor widow who threw in two mites. In verse 42, Jesus used that moment to teach the disciples: "*Assuredly, I say to you that this poor widow has put in more than all those who have given to the treasury; for they all put in out of their abundance, but she out of her poverty put in all that she had, her whole livelihood.*" This was an aha moment.

At one point, Jesus invited Peter to come to Him as He walked on the water. Peter stepped out of the boat into the stormy waters (Matthew 14:25–33). Quickly, that became a teachable moment.

At the Global Institute, we are always looking for teachable moments. We know that even small setbacks can become a helpful teaching aid. Long van rides to and from events or ministry sites offer time to discuss and evaluate our experiences and process what we are learning.

Field Trips

Mark 9:14–29 offers one of many examples of Jesus' discipling style. While Jesus had taken Peter, James, and John on a field trip to a high mountain, He left the other disciples to minister on a different field trip. A boy who was mute due to an evil spirit was brought to them, but they were unable to bring healing to him. When Jesus arrived, the father of the boy told Him of this disappointment. Jesus healed the man's son. Later, in private, the disciples asked him, "Why couldn't we drive it out?" Jesus replied, *"This kind can come out by nothing but prayer."*

This event, also recorded in Luke 9, impacted those disciples. Soon after that incident, in Luke 11:1, they pleaded with Jesus, *"Lord, teach us to pray."* See a connection?

I'm a big fan of taking our young disciples to places where they will encounter other strong believers, but also to places where they will encounter people who have great need. Few things prompt good conversations about life like these occasional outings.

Once, we went to a conference where thousands of young people had gathered in a large arena. I was sitting with our disciple team in the nose-bleed section. Right beside us was a large and very rowdy group of students who seemed to have a hard time staying focused on the speakers far below. They were much more interested in talking and joking with each other. Very distracting.

During a break, one of our students met the youth leader of this group. He asked the youth leader if he was having difficulties with his group. The leader replied, "Oh, you bet, it's like herding cats. But a lot of these kids are not believers . . . yet. We brought them here to meet kids like you who love Jesus." Oh-h-h. Then came the clincher as the youth leader asked my guy, "Oh, and where are *your* lost kids?"

Say wha—?

On the way back home there was an animated conversation among them about how they needed to go out and engage lost students and invite more of them to our youth group. I drove quietly as they discussed this apparently new and revolutionary possibility, thinking, "Isn't this what I have been saying for weeks?" This was like a revelation from God for our guys. And they took it to heart. They began a sort of campaign at their schools to reach out to the rowdies. And it did rock the boat back home at the youth group. But in a good way.

My takeaway from that trip: plan more field trips. Maybe it will be a retreat, a mission project, sports event, or other outings. Get them into situations where they will be confronted with the needs of other people and expose them to the weak areas in their own walk with Jesus. These experiences will help them see their world as Jesus sees it . . . with compassion (Matthew 9:36).

Assignments

Jesus did not hover over His disciples' every move. We know He sent them out in pairs, as He did in Mark 6:7-13. But He also gave them individual tasks. These assignments stretched the disciples' faith. In Matthew 17:24–37, Jesus sent Peter fishing . . . for tax money to pay the authorities! (Lesson: God provides!) He sent two disciples to secure a donkey for Him to ride into the city of Jerusalem. (Lesson: other people are willing to help.) And He sent them to find the place to take the Passover meal. (Lesson: ministry involves menial tasks.) Jesus told the disciples to pray at the Garden of Gethsemane while He went a little farther to pray alone. (Lesson: prayer is imperative.) The assignments were not always clearly spiritual, not even fun, but they pointed to a spiritual imperative.

Just as Jesus gave assignments to His disciples, so should we. And not necessarily glamorous tasks. Anyone who engages in ministry can tell you that most of what we do in ministry is anything but glamorous. Actually, you can discern much about your students' motivation to serve when you invite them to come and help you clean the youth room . . . or your garage. But doesn't that sound kind of self-serving, you say? Nope. It gives you time together with your students. It fosters some deep conversations. It helps them to realize that life is not always glamorous. You have daily chores, just as they should. Who knew? We will discuss the importance of serving others more in Part Five.

Utilizing mundane moments and small tasks will not only contribute to their personal servant spirit. These tasks will also offer life lessons for disciples to help them become self-disciplined toward the larger mission, reaching a lost world with the Gospel of Jesus.

Examinations

Jesus also gave tests! In fact, He often asked questions. There were little quizzes and big exams. One day after Jesus had taught the people who gathered from nearby towns, the disciples reminded Jesus, "*This place is deserted, and it is already late. Send the crowds away so that they can go into the villages and buy food for themselves*" (Matthew 14:15). Those disciples were very insightful, right? Or maybe they were just hungry, tired, and ready to call it a day? Jesus just needed a gentle reminder. Instead, He responded, "*They don't need to go away . . . you give them something to eat*" (Matthew 14:16). Huh? John's account tells us that Jesus asked Philip where to get food "*only to test him*" (John 6:5-6).

We all know what happened next. Jesus produced enough food from five loaves and two fishes to feed the crowd of five thousand men, plus women and children, with twelve baskets left over. But then, Matthew 14:22 tells us, "*Immediately he made the disciples get into the boat and go ahead of him to the other side, while he dismissed the crowds."*

Notice Jesus' mood. The original language indicates that He forced the disciples into the boat. Then He went to the mountain alone to pray. I have been to Galilee, and I wonder if Jesus sat atop Mount Arbel, which overlooks the sea. Beside Arbel is a deep valley leading to the Mediterranean. From there, winds whistle through the canyon onto the Sea of Galilee to whip up whitecaps on the lake. Could Jesus, who commands the wind and the waves, have summoned a storm to stir things up for His disciples out there on the lake?

Then He came to them in the midst of the turbulence, walking on the water. The story, recorded in Mark 6:51–52, relates that Jesus *"got into the boat with them, and the wind ceased. They were completely astounded because they had not understood about the loaves."* They failed the test with the feeding of the five thousand. When they didn't pass the test the first time with the loaves, they got another test. First the bread test, now a water test!

Yet another test came soon in Mark 8 when Jesus fed four thousand. Seven baskets of food were left over. Again, back into the boat. Jesus told the disciples to beware the leaven of the Pharisees. Uh-oh. Was He referring, once again, to the bread lesson from the feeding of the five thousand?

If you were in a boat a second time with Jesus and the subject of bread came up, would you be nervous? Feel the wind picking up, boys?

The disciples discussed this comment among themselves and realized that they had failed to bring enough bread onto the boat. Uh-oh. Jesus, who was listening to their nervous conversation about the bread, asked, in Mark 8:17–18, "*Why are you discussing the fact you have not bread? Don't you understand or comprehend? Do you have hardened hearts? Do you have eyes and not see; do you have ears and not hear? And do you not remember?*"

I can just read their thoughts, or at least mine if I were there: "Remember? Oh, Jesus, do we ever remember that last boat ride . . . if that's what you mean!?"

In Mark 8:20, Jesus asked, "*When I broke the five loaves for the five thousand, how many baskets full of leftovers did you collect? 'Twelve,' they told him. When I broke the seven loaves for the four thousand, how many baskets full of pieces did you collect?*" Sorry to interrupt the story, but can you visualize the side glances here? I can just see everyone turning to Peter! "It is seven, right, Peter? You're the big guy. You tell Him!" "The right answer, Master, is s-s-s-seven?"

"*And he said to them, "Don't you understand yet?*" (Mark 8:21). Yet? Can you not hear the exasperation in His voice? "After two tests with bread and two boat rides, you still don't have the answer? You don't get that I am sufficient for your every need? You don't know that I am trustworthy? I AM the bread, and I am right here in the boat with you morons!" (Okay, I know He didn't say they were morons. But if I had been in the boat that day, I couldn't have faulted Him if He had looked right at me as He said it!)

Jesus did indeed give tests. This made the disciples very nervous. It was good for them to be tested, though, don't you think? Your young disciples will need to be placed in situations where their faith is tested. And yes, this will involve giving them opportunities to fail.

Let me explain. As you navigate young disciples to future leadership roles, they cannot really learn success without tasting the bitterness of a few failures. And I do mean a *few* failures. As I first began to disciple young people, I was guilty of painting whopping pictures of them winning their whole school to Christ. I probably shouldn't have. Sometimes visions can seem too lofty, and goals can become self-defeating.

I learned through trial and error that while we should paint a big picture that is large enough to inspire sacrifice, we also must paint a picture that is small enough to include individual successes, which may seem very small.

Measured risk is a big deal with your student disciples. Give them small tests in the beginning to help them taste what it feels like to win. Instead of urging them to reach all the students they don't know, help them to start by reaching one student they do know.

Is there a bigger win than winning a lost soul to Christ? Evangelism is the topic of Part Four, but I'll go ahead and give you a hint: NO. When your young charges have had the privilege of personally seeing someone's life change before their eyes, the joy of it will be transformative. For the new convert. For the disciple. For your whole youth group! And then, boy, do you ever need to celebrate all those wins whenever they come along! Even a little win is a win worth celebrating! Pizza time! Reward what you want repeated!

Graduation

Just as Jesus brought His discipleship season to a close, you will do the same with your young charges. The parting may be hard. Letting go is the worst. But remember, your job was just preparatory; your challenge was to join with the Holy Spirit as He enabled them to reach the next stage, spiritual Ability. Then, it will be time for them to lead. For His disciples, it was about becoming

Apostles who would start the spread of the Gospel throughout the whole world.

But before the first disciples could lead others, they had yet more lessons to learn about overcoming the evil one. Teaching alone would not be enough. Content needs to be combined with training that will help your disciples develop competencies.

In the very last chapter, we will examine how to determine whether a disciple has truly graduated from the Accountability stage and is ready to move into the role of spiritual father, the Ability stage. We will have more to say about graduation then.

DISCIPLESHIP WILL PRIORITIZE SELF-STUDY SKILLS

We should not lose sight of the end goal in delivering content. We want to develop disciples who desire to grow in their Bible skills. We hope they will pursue the written Word that gives testimony to the Living Word, Jesus. When they dig on their own, they will desire to pass on to others what they are learning.

Let's go back to our passage in 1 John 2:12–14 which describes the three qualities of spiritual youths: they are strong, the word abides in them, and they are overcoming the evil one. Disciples learn to Equip themselves, but not only because they must. Not even because they want to. No, they have learned that they cannot survive—much less serve—apart from a relationship with Jesus through Scripture and prayer.

We help disciples Equip themselves by learning to regularly read and study (not just skim) the Word, by seeking to memorize Scripture, and by constant prayer and meditation on the Word. Let's look at each part of that statement, one phrase at a time.

By learning to regularly read and study (not just skim) the Word.

To be strong, one must eat. Regularly. Isn't that what growing teens do? A disciple is one who has recognized he must feed himself. He shouldn't need nudging or persuasion to eat, nor should he sit in his spiritual highchair waiting for someone else to feed him. He must learn to eat or starve. He must develop an appetite for meat, not milk only (Hebrews 5:11–14).

It is not enough for us to teach. These young disciples must acquire skills to learn for themselves through inductive Bible study methods, etc. We want to see them study, not just skim, the Word.

Perhaps you could consider asking your disciples to read through the New Testament in a semester. Or the entire Bible in a school year. Whatever you ask of them, include clearly defined expectations . . . and some methods, too. Dave Rahn and Ebonie Davis wrote about this: "Engaging is deep-dive worthy, but reading can be a surface experience. Their electronic media deluge has trained them to skim quickly. So, we asked participants to choose at least one of six options to supplement their daily reading: 1) meditate on it, 2) pray over it, 3) talk about it, 4) memorize part of it, 5) write about it, and/or 6) act on it. Each of these qualified as an engagement strategy to help our hearts take a listening posture with God."[13]

Not only that, but we also hope to see an eagerness, even a growing urgency, to pass along to others what they are discovering about God's riches. One way you can help your young disciples to dig deeper in their own study of Scripture is to ask them to teach passages to each other in your disciple meetings. At some point later in your disciple meetings, begin to pass around opportunities for each disciple to share in teaching through a study of one of the

Gospels or the book of Acts, etc. We learn best when we voice what we are digesting by sharing it with others.

If you want to really enhance their learning curve, allow time after their teaching for fellow disciples to critique the lesson. Let disciples share one thing they have learned from the teaching, one thing that they thought the disciple teacher did well, and one thing that could be improved next time. This will help disciples improve their study . . . and their teaching.

By seeking to memorize Scripture.

Perhaps the single most important aspect of Bible intake for disciples is that they are memorizing it. "*Thy word have I hid in my heart that I may not sin against thee*" (Psalm 119:11 KJV). 1 John 2:14 indicates that the Word is not just *on* them, but *in* them! Jesus used words (The Word), not a scroll, to beat off the Devil in the wilderness. Perhaps you could choose a smaller Bible book for disciples to memorize; maybe you could require 3–4 verses per week in bite-size chunks. What an accomplishment that would be! At the Global Institute, students memorize 2 Timothy over two semesters; that book is a great little letter from Paul to his mentee, Timothy.

By constant prayer and meditation on the Word.

Praying is like breathing. You wouldn't want to take only one breath a day, right? Your disciples need to maintain a prayer conversation with Jesus throughout the day. Paul admonished us to pray without ceasing (1 Thessalonians 5:17). Still, taking disciplined time to write down prayers (and answers to prayers) can be a very healthy habit for young disciples to acquire.

Not only that, but disciples must also learn to apply Scriptures carefully to make appropriate application of God's truths in their own lives. Proverbs 4:7 tells us, *"Wisdom is the principal thing; therefore get wisdom. And in all your getting, get understanding."* My friend Randy Smith says of meditating, "You can 'go through' the Bible, but have you allowed the Bible to 'go through' YOU?"

One way to promote their prayer life and meditation on the Word is to teach your disciples to journal their journey daily as part of their quiet time with the Lord. As a college student, I attended a conference where a few of us were assigned to a hotel room with the university dean, Bill Rogers. The dean stayed up for several long minutes after we had gone to bed at night. He turned off all the lights except the one at a small reading desk, then began to write in a notebook.

My curiosity overcame my manners. I asked him what he was writing. He replied, "This is my journal. I record my thoughts about my day, my observations, what I felt I accomplished, my insights from Scripture passages I am reading and memorizing, that sort of thing. Then I write down ideas about what I need to do tomorrow." "Oh," I replied. I didn't ask any more questions. It hadn't occurred to me that keeping a diary was something that grown men did. I wrongly associated the practice with the silly secrets of pre-adolescent girls. But I couldn't get that image of my dean's faithful journaling out of my head.

Later, journaling became a lifelong discipline for me. Journaling helps me to organize my thoughts, reflect on what is happening in my life, and consider how to respond biblically. I gain insight as I take time to write down my thoughts. I would have forgotten so many insights from Scripture and countless life lessons had it not been preserved in writing.

DISCIPLESHIP CAN PRODUCE SELF-DISCIPLINED AND SCRIPTURALLY CONFIDENT DISCIPLES

As we wrap up our discussion regarding disciples' Equipping relationship with Christ, let's summarize the last three chapters. Discipleship begins as we help our disciples to grow in the character of self-discipline intellectually, physically, spiritually, and socially as Jesus did (Luke 2:52). According to 1 John 2:14, disciples must first become strong as they pursue the character of Christ through self-discipline (Heart).

Character counts, and the enemy knows it. Spiritual strength and stamina are required for battle. He will attack at the point of our weakest area of discipline. It is no wonder that spiritual self-discipline is where Satan attacks first and hardest.

Then they pursue Scriptural confidence (Head). Their confidence must be based upon God's Word, not upon feelings or emotions. Praying always, said Paul in Ephesians 6:14-18, we wield our only offensive weapon, the sword of the Spirit, the Word of God.

The enemy will always seek to disarm us. He moves to cut off our communication with our Commander-in-Chief by attacking our two communication tools, Scripture and prayer. This is where the second component, Scriptural confidence, comes into play. Think about it: the Devil relentlessly attacks Scripture. He tries to persuade us that the first book is an unreliable myth, the last book is an unintelligible mystery, and everything in between is an unverifiable mess.

And prayer? Satan whispers that nothing you pray changes anything, that prayer only worked, if at all, for very special Bible characters. But for the rest of us, he intones that prayer consists of meaningless platitudes that begin with "Our most gracious Heavenly Father" and ends with "Amen."

Take away Scripture and prayer and what is left? You know, and so does the Devil. Separated from these—and from Him—we are disarmed, isolated, and powerless. The enemy is fully aware of the danger posed by Spirit-empowered servants who access these two vital resources.

As your disciples gain the first two components, self-disciplined character and Scriptural confidence, they will grow in an intimate relationship with Jesus. Then they are ready to move into the third and final discipleship component, servant leader competencies (Hands). Competencies are related to our disciples' mission with other people and will encompass both their Evangelizing relationships and their Encouraging relationships.

As we are effectively Equipped, we will be ready to tackle the last growth component of discipleship, competency in relating to people through Evangelizing and Encouraging. Becoming Equipped to relate personally with God is our disciples' first and foremost challenge. However, both of the next two relationships (Evangelizing and Encouraging) are about relating with human beings. And that is quite a different challenge! This final component of discipling will take all of Part Four and Part Five to explore.

PART FOUR

SOLDIERS OVERCOMING SATAN

How to Develop Accountability Level Evangelizing

CHAPTER 10

WHO, ME? A SOLDIER? BUT I'M ONLY SIXTEEN!

Helping Disciples Learn How to Overcome

Why would we want to become overcomers, as the Apostle John described it, if we have nothing to overcome? Why would we train if there is no fight? No war? None of the arduous discipleship training would make any sense.

NEWS FLASH: WE ARE AT WAR!

Be assured. There is a war, and believers must choose between being skilled warriors or potential hostages of the enemy. That war begins the moment we receive Christ. We enlist to become part of His Great Commission, to go and make disciples of all nations (Matthew 28:18-20). 1 John 3:8 reminds us that *"The reason the Son of God appeared was to destroy the devil's work."* Jesus said, *"Whoever loses his life for me and for the gospel will save it"* (Mark 8:35).

That sounds like war to me. I know very little about the devastating effects of war, but I have had brief sobering encounters with its effects both in Ukraine and Israel. While I was in Kiev teaching at the seminary, the Russian invasion of Ukraine was imminent. Everyone talked about the precarious situation the country faced. Two weeks after I left the country, Russia invaded. I began to receive heart-rending texts from my new friends there. I felt such pain for their plight. Their homes, their cities, their lives were wrecked by the devastation. However, many around me here at home did not share my newly acquired awareness. Why? For most of my friends, Ukraine was a distant war that had only a minor effect on their daily lives. Not so for me.

And Israel? After the October 7 massacre in 2023, co-workers we had known for years and served with only a few months before were thrown into surreal situations as they cared for displaced and hurting people. We felt all this intensely. But for many, this was not the case.

Isn't this how it works for everyone? We are often only aware of others' pain when it is our friends whose lives have been disrupted by war, sickness, or disasters. If your teens feel unaffected by the raging spiritual battle surrounding them, then perhaps they have been too protected and disengaged, lulled into a spiritual slumber in which the battle seems distant and disconnected.

But the spiritual battle still rages, and when it strikes close to home, they are unprepared. Throughout the Scriptures we see only one objective: the redemption of all God's creation from the ruinous effects of human rebellion against Him. Jesus called the Church to join Him in this all-consuming rescue mission. However, to accomplish that, we must engage—and overcome—the enemy.

THE CONTEST WORTH ENGAGING: ETERNITY AT STAKE

God is love. We will explore this amazing reality later in this chapter. But first, let's tackle another reality. During the past few decades of Church history, "Hell" has nearly disappeared from our spiritual vocabulary. Oh, maybe not in your church. Certainly not from God's Word. Yet, it seems to have quietly vanished in many churches and denominations in recent decades. Old hymns like "Onward Christian Soldiers" seem so yesterday, even inappropriately aggressive. As we have attempted to become more seeker-friendly and attractional to lost people, we have slowly gravitated away from potentially offensive terms and truths embedded in Scripture.

Many believers don't (or won't) talk about sin much anymore. Gary Vander Wiele wrote, "We have reached a point in a culture wherein . . . many people, especially students, tend to respond to discussions of sin with a knowing eye roll or a shoulder shrug. Most students we encounter will have some understanding of what sin is, but they will dismiss the conversation out of hand because they either think that they're not that bad or that sin isn't real or relevant."[14] Perhaps this is not so with your students, but it is widespread in many churches, even denominations.

Jesus died for our sin! Clearly, it was a big deal to Him. Oddly, it is Jesus who is offensive to many who are oblivious to their sin and unaware of sin's consequences. He is *"Christ crucified: a stumbling block to Jews and foolishness to Gentiles"* (1 Corinthians 1:23). We have preached a Gospel of love to the near exclusion of Hell on the grounds that Jesus was all about love. While it is true that God *is* love, this lop-sided approach conveniently ignores His purpose. Jesus—love personified—went to Calvary to defeat the enemy and rescue us from eternal separation from God. Oh, and this was a separation of our own making because of our arrogant rebellion. Wow!

Where does sin lead? Isaiah 59:2 says, *"Your iniquities have made a separation between you and your God."* There is a great gulf between us and a holy God. If unbelievers insist upon separating from God, He will one day grant their wish once and for all, which is what they insisted upon, at times emphatically. He respects their decision; He will not always strive with man (Genesis 6:3).

God's love is powerful and attractive; we will explore that in more depth later in this chapter. But, as we discussed in Chapter Eight, we cannot promote God's love apart from the reality of God's law. For His love to have meaning, we cannot avoid discussions about sin. After all, if there is no bad news (Hell), then who needs Good News (salvation)? If there is no Hell and God freely forgives everyone for their rebellion whether they repent or not, then we no longer have the free will to resist Him. But isn't Heaven about an actual choice to be with a Person (God), *not* only about being in a place with gold streets or huge mansions? Those who reject God would be confined to be with Him forever under His authority, precisely what they sought to escape. What kind of Heaven would that be?

God does not ignore justice. But His love, embodied in Jesus' cherished words in John 3:16, has no imperative for anyone apart from His just sentence of condemnation in John 3:17-18. The Gospel has no meaning (or urgency) if we are not being saved from the just penalty we deserve.

Isn't it interesting that people are so into justice these days? It is deeply embedded in our nature, a reflection of our Maker who made us in His image. People hit the streets to demand justice for all manner of perceived "woke" injustices like gender issues, reparations for slavery, women's reproductive rights, and environmental concerns. Anyone opposed must be canceled. People cannot abide the idea of no justice for sinners, especially those we perceive to have sinned against us! But we want mercy or even absolution for our own sin. Interesting how that works. We bristle against God's justice for our rebellion against His holiness, paid in full in our behalf at the Cross by His one and only Son. But we insist on our own odd mix of selective justice. Wrapped in self-righteous indignation, we insist upon redemption for us and retribution for them. To be honest, it seems that the Church has been very hesitant to speak of God's justice in recent decades. Perhaps the secular world feels the need to fill the vacuum left by our silence?

THE COMBATANTS WHO WAGE THIS EPIC CONTEST

Who is the Enemy?

Paul identifies the real enemy: "*For we do not wrestle against flesh and blood, but against principalities, against powers, against the rulers of the darkness of this age, against spiritual hosts of wickedness in the heavenly places*" (Ephesians 6:12). Clearly, the real enemy is Satan. Not other people.

Humanity has been Satan's prime target since the beginning. Many people have been "*taken captive by him* (Satan) *to do his will*" (2 Timothy 2:26). The Bible makes it clear that Satan is already defeated and ultimately will be cast into the "lake of fire." Then why this war? Satan's fight is with God. But humanity, God's crowning creation, makes an easy target. Satan aims to frustrate God's plan to restore harmony with His Creation. In John 10:10,

Jesus told us that Satan is a thief who comes to *"steal, and to kill, and to destroy."* He is playing for keeps. C.S. Lewis said, "There is no neutral ground in the universe; every square inch, every split second is claimed by God and counterclaimed by Satan."[15] Does that sound like a battle?

Who are the Soldiers?

Against the grim backdrop of this cosmic battle, what is our task with young disciples? God has engaged believers to join His great rescue operation. We must prepare them to bravely take His light into darkness to find and rescue the lost. *"But you are a chosen race, a royal priesthood, a holy nation, a people for his own possession, that you may proclaim the excellencies of him who called you out of darkness into his marvelous light"* (1 Peter 2:9). Paul wrote in 2 Timothy 2:3, *"Join with me in suffering, like a good soldier of Christ Jesus."* Does that seem ambiguous? We are engaged in a conflict with the evil one to rescue those he has taken captive.

When your disciples tell people that we are all sinners in need of a Savior, this news may not be well received. If anyone thinks they can escape danger while sharing that news, they should read Jesus' words in John 15:18-19. He was hated because He pointed out the problem of human sin. Bringing light to the darkness is like turning on a light in a dark room! Ouch! Jesus said that we are salt. Salt on an open wound brings a strong reaction! Why would we be surprised at this?

Jesus never doubted His mission or underestimated the enemy that He was preparing His disciples to engage. Their job was to share God's love with the whole world. They would have to overcome the enemy. Discipleship was the means He gave us to prepare believers to win. Discipleship was a starting point for the rescue mission, not just a means of self-improvement.

Youth ministry that hopes to reach young people with the Gospel must begin with students themselves. In a football game, no one can play except the team. The opposition won't play for the team. The officials cannot. The crowd came to watch, not play. Not even the coach or any of the coaching staff can take the field to carry the ball. The only people who can face the opposing team are the team players. In youth ministry, only the youth themselves can carry the ball.

Sometimes youth groups don't embrace a motivating purpose, a process to fulfill it, or a product to achieve at the end of it. Rather, the focus is on meeting the felt needs only of those who attend. It may seem that the goal is to keep the children of church members off the street and out of trouble. You know, good—not godly— kids. In that scenario, spiritual depth is nice but not necessary. In fact, engaging teens in the pursuit of God's transformational spiritual purpose may be viewed as undesirable, dangerous, and even radical in some congregations. (Gasp here.)

The result of such a protective church environment for teenagers is that it may only coddle the least mature levels of spiritual growth while discouraging growth for teens who may be ready for a greater challenge. Ultimately, when we do not provide that opportunity, we will stymie and then kill growth, both spiritual and numerical.

It is imperative for our students to view themselves as Christ's team in their community. They must learn to take the initiative to win their world to Christ. Francis Shaefer wrote, "We as Bible-believing evangelical Christians are locked in a battle. This is not a friendly gentleman's discussion. It is a life and death conflict between the spiritual hosts of wickedness and those who claim the name of Christ."[16]

Unfortunately, many students have never acknowledged that winning the lost in their community is their unique ministry. It has simply never occurred to them that their peers are their personal responsibility, their mission field—much less a battlefield.

For many years, frankly, neither did I. In fact, I assumed that since I was the youth minister, the school campus was *my* mission field. However, when I arrived to assume my duties at Trinity Church in San Antonio, Texas, I quickly realized the folly of this approach. My previous church had students attending three or four area schools. Most attended the same one. Visiting those schools was comparatively easy. But students at this church attended over thirty middle schools and high schools across the city and in neighboring towns. The number of schools and the distance between them was a crushing weight. I couldn't get around to all those schools in several weeks of visits! In some schools, I wasn't even welcome. Thanks, drug peddlers.

So, what was I to do? I tried to visit as many campuses, football games, recitals, and other school events as I could. But my efforts were too thin and too spread out. Then I tried to focus on just the six or seven schools where most of our young people attended. That did not work well either, as it seemed to overlook many youth members who attended other schools.

Overwhelmed, I told God that it would be impossible for me to reach the lost kids on all those campuses. Ha. I believe He allowed me to go through that pain to teach me an important lesson.

It began to sink into my spirit that while I could spend only an hour or two per week on any of their campuses, the students were there for forty hours a week! This was their battlefield, not mine. Okay, I know that all of this is obvious to you. But it wasn't to me, at least not until then. Jesus sent His disciples on a great mission. So should we.

The next summer at youth camp, after I finished teaching our older teens about the importance of their personal witness among their peers, a group of them gathered around me. They asked, "Glidewell, you have been telling us to be a witness to our neighbors, our football team, our high school buddies, and our beer-drinking, girl-crazy friends. We are ready. What is the plan?"

Plan? In truth, I had spent weeks preparing these camp lessons. But when they responded with eager anticipation, I realized that I had not given them a plan that was simple or specific. I guess I thought they would go back to their homes and schools with no plan but get a different result. That sounds like the proverbial definition of insanity. These students were telling me that they were ready to take the field of battle. The trouble was, they had no plan and neither did I.

The Real Soldiers

The next week, after agonized prayer, I called those students together and said, "I have an answer to your question at camp. I am resigning . . . as your school's campus minister. I'm appointing each of you as the campus minister of your school. Whatever God chooses to do on your campus, He is far more likely to do it through you than through me. It is time for you to consider yourselves the designated—whether recognized or unrecognized—ministers to your campuses and communities as Christ's ambassadors. If this city's teens are to hear the Gospel, you must assume that it is your responsibility. Let's discover together what His marching orders will be in each of your ministries." Basically, this gave them clear permission to claim their battlefield.

That was the beginning of something that I can hardly describe in one book, much less one chapter! When those young people realized that they had been commissioned to reach their fellow students on their school campuses with the light and love of Christ, something happened among them. Suddenly, they had a clear objective, a mission! And what happened next transformed our youth group. If your disciples grasp this, it will change everything for them.

Is Youth Ministry For Us Or By Us?

When it finally dawned on me that youth ministry should not forever be *for* students (by me, the youth leader), but should be *by* students *for* others, this started a complete revolution in our ministry. This "by us" level of ministry is one which many youth groups never attain. In fact, it may not ever even be offered to them. And that, frankly, is tragic. They were meant to win.

How are your young disciples to win this war? As I detailed in my book, *ReGroup*, Availability level group service projects and outreach events provide a pathway to help teens engage this battle together as a group. However, these provide only a first step. While such activities are good, they are just not good enough—not for the long-term strategy to win the war against the enemy. They are more like skirmishes than a sustained assault on enemy strongholds. We must do more. The next step is individual witness, a far more daunting prospect to many students.

THE COMPASSION THAT PRECEDES GOSPEL CONVERSATIONS

How do we prepare student disciples to Evangelize individually? We cannot send them as soldiers to war without being properly Equipped. Paul wrote, *"For though we walk in the flesh, we do not war according to the flesh. For the weapons of our warfare are not carnal but mighty in God for pulling down strongholds, casting down arguments and every high thing that exalts itself against the knowledge of God"* (2 Corinthians 10:3–5).

Pulling down strongholds? Casting down arguments? Won't we need some heavy artillery for that task? I'm picturing spiritual tanks rolling across enemy lines blowing everything to bits!

But wait. Is that the idea behind Evangelism? Are we talking street demonstrations, big signs bearing the inscription Turn or Burn, and militant believers shouting down other people's arguments? One might think so, based on depictions by the media in recent years. The news outlets have loved to feature believers who march down the street to protest gay rights or shout through megaphones at pro-choice rallies, etc. These selective depictions paint all Christians with one brush, as Neanderthals with big sticks, haters who run at those they dislike to rain down heavenly fire on sinners with hateful words. But that is not the picture we get from Jesus or the Gospels. In the Bible we are far more likely to find that it is the believers who are being persecuted, beaten, stoned, tortured, whipped, and left for dead. Or crucified.

A Most Unexpected Weapon!

Jesus had compassion for the lost (Matthew 9:36). Like Him, we have one weapon: God's love. (I noted that we would take up this amazing attribute again in this chapter!) Against the black backdrop of human sin (we had to start there), His love shines like a guiding star. In Acts 1:8 we are assured that we would receive power. But power for what? Wait for it: *"And you shall be my witnesses."* His love is not just for us but moves through us to touch others, leading us to love even our enemies. Such love is supernatural! Romans 5:8 reminds us that *"while we were still sinners, Christ died for us."* This is no "shrinking violet" kind of love. There is no force more powerful than God's love. Love is patient but never passive or weak. Jesus' love is kind, but also powerful and bold, facing down the Devil at the Cross and storming the gates of Hell.

In Galatians 5:22–23, the nature of God's compassion is described: *"But the fruit of the Spirit is love, joy, peace, longsuffering, kindness, goodness, faithfulness, gentleness, self-control. Against such there is no law."* All those virtues are really attributes of the first, love. God's love is not natural; it is supernatural. The only source for such love is God Himself.

You are training your disciples to go to war against Satan, armed with the Sword of the Spirit to combat him. But we do not bash hurting and blinded people over the head with a Bible. Instead, we offer the lifeline of God's love, described in His Word and available by His Spirit.

The idea of disciples lobbing fruit—you know, like apples and peaches—to explode over barriers thrown up by the enemy sounds ridiculous, I know. Instead, like fruit on a tree, the spiritual fruit listed in Galatians 5 is what will draw inquisitive, hungry people to us! I mean, who wouldn't want some of that? 1 Peter 3:15 reminds us that God's love attracts people to us: *"Always be prepared to give an answer to everyone who asks you to give the reason for the hope that you have."*

Love is a powerful force; it utilizes supernatural rather than mere mortal strength. Does that change the battle plan for you? Are you leading your disciples to understand that they have a mighty weapon against the powers of darkness? That it will pull down rebel strongholds where brute force could not? That the futile arguments of logic and reason people throw up to insulate themselves from the pain of their emptiness come tumbling down when the Holy Spirit convicts them of God's love, demonstrated at the Cross?

God's love is not remote, aloof, or reserved in Heaven. His love came down to earth wrapped in human flesh to take the blows for our rebellion, yet cried out, "Father, forgive them." At the Cross, God's nature was on full display to all, the ultimate proof of God's love. As Christ's ambassadors, we are called to demonstrate that same love to a cynical, hating, frightened world.

Yes, we fight off the Devil with the "sword of the Spirit" (Ephesians 6:13-18). But we win souls with the fruit of the Spirit, God's love. It is amazing to see God's compassionate love work through His people to bring about extraordinary transformation in other people's lives.

As God's love flows into us, it then must flow out from us. Why? Because God in us cannot be contained. Witnessing is not something your disciples will do because they must, or even because they want to. They will share God's love with other people because, as Peter told the Sanhedrin in Acts 4:20, they can't help it! His love overflows from them because His love is greater, larger than they can contain. It (He) must come out! So, they speak of it because *the mouth speaks what the heart is full of* (Luke 6:45). The love of Christ, said Paul, compels them to pursue a ministry of reconciliation (2 Corinthians 5:12-21).

In fact, you will know discipleship is working if your disciples Evangelize! Even in dangerous circumstances, faithful believers have uttered the name of Jesus under threat of imprisonment, torture, or even death. Matthew 10:19–20 says, *"But when they arrest you, do not worry about what to say or how to say it. At that time you will be given what to say, for it will not be you speaking, but the Spirit of your Father speaking through you."* The Spirit will give your disciples courage, boldness, and presence of mind. They cannot help but speak, moved by His love.

In a blog titled "The Most Important Metric," Ken Adams wrote: "Now, let's define a fully trained disciple of Jesus Christ. A fully trained disciple is a person who demonstrates growth in the character of Christ as described in Galatians 5:22–23 in the fruit of the Spirit. If a person is becoming more like Christ in the way that person displays love, joy, peace, patience, kindness, goodness, gentleness, faithfulness, and self-control, then that person is becoming fully trained."[17] The Spirit's compassion and love flowing through your disciples is a powerful witness.

THE CONDUCT THAT PROMPTS GOSPEL CONVERSATIONS

We must move our disciples beyond group Evangelism activities such as service projects and outreach events (both good activities, described in my book *ReGroup*) to individual verbal witness. We begin by Equipping disciples in their relationship with Jesus. Then we engage them in a two-fold strategy, including both external and internal measures. Externally, we rescue lost souls (Evangelizing). Internally, we strengthen the Body for battle (Encouraging) as Paul instructs us in Ephesians 4:12. These two relationships are the subjects of the rest of this book.

For many congregations, engaging teens in group service projects is fine. But personal Evangelism? Speaking Jesus' name? Too confrontational. That type of spiritual engagement is way too aggressive, at least for teenagers, right? This protective sentiment, though not vocalized as such, assumes that teenagers are not ready for "that kind of Evangelism."

Really? Several of Jesus' disciples were likely only teenagers while Jesus was training them to become bold witnesses for the Gospel. I hate to break it to you, but the final mark of a spiritual "young man" in 1 John 2:12–14 is that he is *"overcoming the evil one."* Does that sound dangerous? It should. This war will continue until Jesus returns. Our disciples must determine whether they will become the victors or the vanquished. Paul wrote in Romans 10:14, *"How can they hear without someone preaching to them?"* He reminded us in 2 Timothy 4:2 to *"preach the word; be prepared in season and out of season."* This requires fully armed, better trained believers. 1 Peter 5:8–9 says, *"Be alert and of sober mind. Your enemy the devil prowls around like a roaring lion looking for someone to devour. Resist him, standing firm in the faith, because you know that the family of believers throughout the world is undergoing the same kind of sufferings."* I've been told that Scripture reminds us to "fear not" at least 365 times, one for every day of the year! Disciples will need at least one of those reminders every single day.

There are books and study materials available to help with this, many designed especially for teenagers. As disciplers, we must help our students embrace the vital role of the Spirit in all their relationships: in Equipping (spiritual power), in Evangelizing (spiritual fruit), and in Encouraging (spiritual gifts).

The Battle Belongs to The Lord

Spoiler alert: Before we go any further, let's catch a glimpse of our coming victory over these dark forces. Jesus said, *"In the world you will have tribulation; but be of good cheer, I have overcome the world"* (John 16:33). Saints win. Satan loses. End of story.

Your disciples can take heart even when enshrouded by dark clouds of despair. In Romans 8:31, Paul spoke eloquently of the battle we face: *"What then shall we say to these things? If God is for us, who can be against us?"* Verses 35–37 continue, *"Who shall separate us from the love of Christ? Shall tribulation, or distress, or persecution, or famine, or nakedness, or peril, or sword? As it is written: 'For your sake we are killed all day long; we are accounted as sheep for the slaughter.'"* But wait! Paul finishes, *"Yet in all these things we are more than conquerors through Him who loved us."*

Frankly, the most dangerous thing you can do is to overprotect your young disciples from engaging the enemy in this great cause. He doesn't quit just because they won't engage. No, he loves that even more; then he can easily devour them. Prepare your disciples for battle!

With all this in mind, let's survey the battlefield.

CHAPTER 11

THE WORLD'S MOST STRATEGIC BATTLEFIELD

How to Help Disciples to Engage the Next Generation

Make no mistake: the enemy has this young generation of believers in his sights. They represent a great potential threat to him, both now and in the future. Thus, their pictures are on wanted posters all over Hell. By all accounts, he seems to be a pretty good marksman.

Unfortunately, instead of strengthening our youth for the battle they are facing, we seem to have made Satan's job far easier for him in recent history. How, you ask?

- We have warehoused young people together in facilities we call "public schools" due to the Industrial Revolution when both parents began to leave the farm to work in the city. Bear in mind that for centuries before that, young people were raised mostly in rural settings, taught daily by their parents who worked side by side with the children to carry out household chores or farmwork. Now, an increasingly centralized educational system has at least partially replaced parents as the primary instructors of the young. Centralized school authorities often indoctrinate young minds with values that are antithetical to biblical morals. This includes LGBTQ, pro-choice, CRT, and more. In some cases, teachers have openly promoted transgender ideology and even aided students in taking life-altering drugs without parental consent.

- We have put devices like cell phones into our children's hands—often unmonitored by adult oversight—that allows instant access to knowledge that not only includes porn but also access to killer drugs like fentanyl. Moreover, we have also served to make them independent of adult instruction. After all, they can access any information they need in seconds now; who needs adults? And now, artificial intelligence (AI) is making its way into their lives!

- We have systematically lowered moral and legal standards to the point that almost anything goes. Extreme individual rights have eclipsed the community good. "Freedom" has been redefined as "freedom from responsibility," or even "my freedom at your expense." We have elevated feelings over facts. Employers are reaping the nightmare of entitled young employees who are ill-prepared for employment. Worse, certain segments of the population are choosing not to work, including thousands of employable young men who have elected to remain in their parents' basements while engaging in online gaming for the equivalent of a full-time job. In some places we are even incentivizing people to not work by offering government-sponsored financial payoffs. We have removed consequences for bad behavior in schools, the judicial system, and even at home.

- We have created medical nightmares at both individual and societal levels. We have medicated teenagers for ADHD to the point that some are unable to socially interact appropriately with others apart from their meds. Many teens rank very low in their emotional quotient (EQ). The COVID-19 pandemic isolated young people and left them without supervision, alone, and reaching out for help in all the wrong places.

What are the results of all this societal re-engineering in teens' lives? The statistics are grim.

- Suicides and hospitalizations for suicide attempts rose 51% among teenage girls after 2020.[18] Along with anxiety and depression, the Covid epidemic greatly escalated this among all teens.
- Alcohol and drug abuse of all kinds: Fentanyl-related deaths have skyrocketed.[19] Opioid abuse is off the charts. The use of prescription drugs for ADHD and other teen maladies has become a go-to remedy. We are the most medicated generation in history. It is unclear how much of this is related to emotional abuse and other deeper issues.
- Dietary problems: Gluten, peanut allergies, lactose intolerance, etc., have crippled a generation of kids with dietary maladies which has affected normal immunity to diseases.
- Mass shootings: One statistic emerged recently stating that 82% of all teenage mass shooters are fatherless young men.[20]

The list could go on, and reams of research have been produced in recent years to detail the disastrous results of these cultural upheavals. The cultural experimentation now underway is unparalleled and has produced mammoth changes in a relatively short time in history.

Despite these realities, has the Church still failed to recognize that there is a war for the hearts of our young people? We may vaguely acknowledge that there is a battle. However, at times it seems that in the midst of this war we have created a playground in the church's youth room to protect students from the battleground beyond its doors! How do we refocus on the mission?

THE BATTLEGROUND DISCIPLES MUST CLAIM

Believers have responded in various ways to culture's increasingly chaotic environment. Many have withdrawn from public schools, leaving the system to move even more rapidly downward into chaos. We get it: for many people and in many demographics, withdrawal may appear to be the only sane alternative that seems available to concerned believers.

However, I would ask, how did we get here? How did we get to the point where it seems that the only alternative left is to withdraw from many cultural arenas like sports, the movie industry, media sources, civic dialogue, etc.? Why has the Church seemingly gone AWOL?

Did we become complacent over time, assuming that the Christian principles that governed our culture for centuries would continue on, unchanged . . . and unchallenged? As the enemy stealthily gained traction in these areas, what did we do? Instead of taking a stand, many believers have retreated from the battlefield to such an extent that Satan is now running roughshod over many young innocents. We have fled the battlefield, hoping to find sanity and safety inside our church houses from an increasingly hostile culture.

Instead of permeating the culture, we have come dangerously close to becoming our own isolated subculture.

The battleground of the political arena is where some people have chosen to engage. I wholeheartedly agree that we have an inescapable civic responsibility to engage our culture. We may admire the bold courage of the cultural warriors, but . . .

But these strategies are insufficient. While the battle rages on many fronts, there is only one solution: Jesus alone convicts and converts hearts, one individual life at a time. Ultimately, victory will come from the inside out, not the other way around.

Jesus recognized different levels of spiritual growth. The Twelve began their relationship with Jesus while still part of the crowds. But later they became more than followers; by their own choice, they became His disciples. A different deal altogether! Discipleship was always our only biblical course of action against Satan. How else would we prepare young believers to fight?

THE BRIDGE DISCIPLES MUST CROSS

Just to be clear, Jesus did not separate Himself from the common people, even those whose lifestyles were openly sinful. He did not advocate isolating His disciples—or Himself—from everyday people as the Pharisees did. He did not remain insulated or aloof from the lost, retreating into the synagogue; He even attended parties hosted by sinners.

Horrors, you say! (With accompanying echoes from the parent chambers.) Surely, you do not mean to say that we should send our young people to associate with sinners, much less to attend their worldly parties?! Well, my answer is no and yes.

No, I do not believe that we should send our young people unprepared to deal with secular society. But yes, we must train young people how to overcome darkness with light. We cannot train them effectively in a highly insulated, sanitized environment. By over-protecting our young people, are we not admitting defeat from the start?

We should be teaching our young disciples how to be *in* the world without being *of* the world. In John 17:16–18, Jesus said: "*They are not of the world, even as I am not of it. Sanctify them by the truth; your word is truth. As you sent me into the world, I have sent them into the world.*"

Preparing Disciples for Effective Evangelism

Jesus said, "Go" but we seem to warn teens, "Don't go!" How odd. Young disciples must learn how to be in their world yet distinctive from it. Contact without contamination. That spiritual enterprise is essential for their own spiritual survival, and for their witness to their world. After all, light does not mix with darkness; rather, it overcomes and dispels it!

The relationship in view in Evangelism is with the secular world, to show and share the love of Christ with those who do not know Him. The Spirit convicts and converts lost souls. It is not our job to save anyone, only to share God's love with them. That can be done right where they are, in their daily lives. Your task is to help your disciples get ready to engage beyond the church walls.

They must resolve to become the overcomers, not the overwhelmed.

Disciples need to prepare to win. How? I suggest that "personal mission ministry" will move students beyond the relative safety of group service projects and outreach events that we described in my previous book, *ReGroup*, about Availability level Evangelism. This next challenge involves a more individual mission field at places and times and in activities where non-believers are already present. Disciples will develop meaningful relationships there with their unchurched peers who are not in places or events that are sponsored by the Church. Your disciples should learn to make friends and to share hope with unsaved youth in situations where they already encounter them in daily life.

Disciples need to learn to get fellow teenagers' attention by paying attention to others' needs. We hope non-believers will begin to *"ask a reason for the hope that is within"* your disciples (1 Peter 3:15). Then they will have something to tell them, something that makes all the difference.

Purpose of a Personal Mission Field Ministry

Why should we prepare young disciples to engage in a more personal witness strategy? There is a Scriptural basis for this approach. Jesus Himself often engaged individuals as He went about the countryside meeting people wherever they were, even lepers and tax collectors. Paul also demonstrated this approach very ably as he went from town to town, often speaking first to individuals like Lydia in Acts 16:14.

This more personal mission field ministry is about helping your disciples to engage with their unchurched peers. That will involve risk and actions that will challenge their safe anonymity. They will need to learn skills like:

- Identifying with peers on their turf, not just at church events.

DYNAMIC DISCIPLESHIP

- Building bridges of friendship with unchurched acquaintances.
- Demonstrating Christ's love for all people.
- Winning the right to be heard by their peers.

What does it look like to engage your disciples in a more individual type of Evangelism ministry? Whether your teens are in public school, private school, or homeschool, they all can—no, must—adopt a mission field, a battlefield. They can all find a ministry among their neighborhood friends, relatives, locker mates, classmates, workmates, online friends or gamers, and sports teams, to name a few.

Prioritizing Personal Mission Field Ministry

One of the greatest advantages of individual witness ministry is that it helps to bring focus to students who may feel overwhelmed by the sheer number of people who need to hear the Gospel. After all, some students attend schools that have a student population in the thousands. When youth leaders instruct youth to reach their schools for Christ, students' eyes may glaze over. They wonder how in the world they are even supposed to make a dent in the darkness they encounter every single day in their school and community.

Add to that the problems created by the increasing effects of social distancing and social media isolation, and you have a challenge on your hands. Many teenagers today simply do not know how to connect with others in any meaningful or personal way. They will need help.

To address this, we ask our disciples to start with just three to five friends or acquaintances to serve as their own mission field.

180

- Perhaps they will begin to pray for one or two students with whom they have a casual relationship, asking Jesus to help them embrace His Spirit of compassion. Just pray!
- There may be one or two others with whom they will engage by specific, regular acts of kindness.
- Finally, they might choose one student (at a time) with whom they are seeking opportunities to start a conversation about Jesus, the source of real hope.

By taking these steps, the goal to reach their mission field becomes more real and achievable, one incremental step at a time.

Places of Personal Mission Field Ministry

Where are some places to engage in personal ministry? Well, any place where teenagers gather, such as athletic events, swimming pools, malls, work, or the school hallway between classes. The people seated around them in their classes may provide a rich mission field. Help your students think through all the places where they are in contact with fellow teens other than at church. Challenge them to seek new opportunities to serve others beyond their current context. Ask them to begin a list of acquaintances who are unchurched.

Practical Steps to Start a Personal Mission Field Ministry

It is important to keep the goal in view for young disciples to help their peers see and hear of God's love for them. Peter tells us in 1 Peter 2:12 to *"live such good lives among the pagans that, though they accuse you of doing wrong, they may see your good deeds and glorify God on the day he visits us."* This is a great initial way to bring the Good News to others as we are led by the Holy Spirit. Some ways your disciples could establish a personal mission ministry might include:

- Being present at events that are important to peers, such as sports events, club meetings, swim meets, plays, etc., events in which they may or may not be a participant.
- Engaging with peers in social and recreational activities, both personally and on social media.
- Getting involved with non-believing youth in activities that they enjoy, like weight lifting, tennis, shopping, gaming, movies, etc.
- Taking time to be helpful and encouraging to individuals.
- Engaging where appropriate with a biblical perspective in conversations about social issues that concern your peers, such as poverty, racism, environment, crime, etc.

Also, older youth may engage in valuable service to other young people such as tutoring, offering a ride to school or church meetings, running errands together, and the like.

Serving others was a primary focus of Jesus' discipleship training. He demonstrated incremental Evangelism to His disciples as He spoke with crowds and individuals. Frankly, so must we. Bible scholars have recounted the many instances in which Jesus engaged people individually. The woman at the well in John 4 and Zacchaeus in Luke 19 quickly come to mind. He often began with a simple question to start a conversation.

How does this apply? When we meet with our disciple group, we should lead them to focus on the mission of Evangelism as Jesus did. Perhaps you can help them by sharing ideas that will bridge the gap with their peers in their own personal ministry.

A youth leader friend of mine brought out a basket and asked his student disciples to write down possible individual acts of service on slips of paper and place them in the basket. Each week, a disciple member drew out one task that they would all attempt to accomplish during the next week and report on people's responses. These pre-Evangelism projects included actions like the ones below:

- Sit in the school cafeteria at a different table to converse with a person outside their friend circles.
- Compliment someone for an achievement, an act of kindness, etc.
- Pray with and for a stranger or fellow student at the store, the gym, school, or elsewhere.
- Send a text or a note of appreciation to a fellow student.
- Host a game night or movie night at your home for a few friends and acquaintances.
- Offer to help a friend or neighbor with a task.
- Add another teen acquaintance to your social media contacts as a route to further engagement.
- Point out a friend's action or attitude you have observed that you admire or hope to emulate.
- Offer a snack or soda to an acquaintance or neighbor.
- Assist a schoolmate with preparation for a project or studying for a test.

Your disciples can add to the list of possibilities. Activities such as these pave the way for new friendships and Spirit-led opportunities to share the love of Christ with new people.

Above all, your disciples must learn how to tell their own story (testimony) in thirty seconds, two minutes, or longer, to fit varying situations that might arise. Let them practice sharing their testimonies with each other. You want them to always be prepared to share (1 Peter 3:15).

Precaution for Effective Personal Mission Field Ministry

Jesus provided an example of how to go into new situations; He took His disciples with Him to heathen environments. Jesus knew that the disciples, whom He would later send into uncertain circumstances, would need to learn the value of mutual support.

Whenever your disciples take God's light into the secular world's activities, they should, at the very least, enlist prayer support from their fellow disciples. You might consider pairing them up, at least in the beginning stages. This helps them in two ways. First, it helps them stay pure because they have made themselves responsible and accountable to other disciples who remind them of their purpose. Even text support is better than no support at all.

Second, this helps them to take a stronger stand for what is right, even in less-than-ideal environments. They can more easily stand when they stand together, either by prayer support and/or personal presence of fellow disciples. After all, we are not talking about asking students to bring lost friends to the church; we are talking about them moving out into a lost and sometimes hostile world (go and tell, not come and see).

Of course, we can never use witnessing as an excuse to partake in worldly behavior. Jesus' motive in every situation was to communicate the Father's love. Nowhere is it recorded that Jesus went to a secular party just to kick back with the boys. He did not go to secular parties to enjoy the band or relax or escape or to try to get His mind off His troubles. He always went with a clear purpose: to share the love of God with those who did not know.

Relaxation, rest, and fellowship were reserved for other settings apart from the crowds. Intentionality is vital.

Whenever your disciples go into a secular environment, their motive should be to help people to know Christ. If this is not their purpose, yet they go knowing that they are unable to resist temptations inherent in a situation, they court disaster in their spiritual walk.

Unleash God's Army!

To accomplish this, according to James 4:7, they must resist the devil, and then he will flee. Jesus told Peter, "*On this rock I will build my church. And the gates of Hades will not overcome it*" (Matthew 16:18). Gates? As a young teen, I imagined Satan's army carrying gates with which to bash Christians. I missed the point of that imagery, that Hell is on the defensive against the Church that marches victoriously into battle against the forces of darkness. The proper picture of Satan's forces? They are being forced to retreat from the battlefield, chased behind the confining gates of Hell. They cannot withstand the irresistible force of God's army.

So, what are we waiting for? Jesus told His disciples to "go!" We must enable our young disciples to do battle with the forces of darkness to rescue the perishing. When they finally realize this is their mission, you will unleash an army that cannot be overcome. Instead, they will be overcomers. Revelation 12:11 says, "*They triumphed over him by the blood of the Lamb and by the word of their testimony; they did not love their lives so much as to shrink from death.*"

Historically, the Church has overcome by its testimony, a testimony of love. We have not, and we must not, shrink from the battlefield.

Taking a stand against the enemy is vital to the mission, the great rescue operation to retake lives that have become ensnared by the Devil.

PART FIVE

SERVANTS OF THE SAINTS

How to Develop Accountability Level Encouraging

CHAPTER 12

DISCIPLES FINDING THEIR PLACE

Disciples Learning How to Serve Others

It's time to shift gears, moving from our external relationships with the world, fulfilling the Great Commission, to our internal relationships within the Church, the "Great Community." Chapter Six gave an overview of the three essential relationships mentioned in Ephesians 4:12. We have explored two: first, our relationship with God (Equipping) which leads to our second relationship with lost people estranged from God (Evangelizing). Now let's focus on our third relationship, the Church (Encouraging). We become Equipped through self-discipline and Scriptural confidence to become competent both in Evangelizing and Encouraging.

Let's zoom out to begin with the bigger picture. Why do we even need the Church? Isn't Jesus enough? Within every human heart, there is a desperate need to belong. We were created for relationship by God who is relational even within Himself as God the Father, the Son, and the Holy Spirit. He made us in His image, creating us for relationship, too. We instinctively know that we are not independent, needing no one. Since we are incomplete within ourselves, we seek companionship to alleviate the pain of our felt aloneness. Larry Crabb wrote, "Because God is in His very nature a relational being . . . man, created to be like God, is also a relational being. We have been built for relationship with God and with other people. It follows that in the most central part of our being, we long to enjoy what we were designed to experience. We long for relationship."[21] Jesus said, *"By this everyone will know that you are My disciples, if you love one another"* (John 13:25). Our love for one another is our ID to the world and critical to our success.

SERVING THE CHURCH BODY IS ESSENTIAL

Our young disciples need to thrive in the fellowship of believers, not just now as teenagers, but always. Hebrews 10:24 says, *"And let's consider how to encourage one another in love and good deeds."* The word "Encourage" does not mean mere surface-level verbal affirmation. It means to instill courage, or as Hal Kitchings explained, "to pound courage into someone."[22] Hmmm, why would we need to instill courage in fellow believers?

We know, of course! There is a war going on out there, and we are the soldiers. In verse 25, "the Day" will bring an end to all wars when Jesus returns. But now the church house serves as a base camp where believers are continually outfitted for battle against the evil one to rescue those taken captive by him before the Day arrives. This battle requires courage. We need each other, just as any foot soldier knows. We need trustworthy people to watch our backs on the battlefield.

During the Vietnam War, soldiers were keenly aware of the anti-war demonstrations going on back home. When they were on leave or had finished their service, they returned to an environment in which many of them were mocked and rejected. Some struggled to find a job. They had been fighting for their country, but their country, it seemed, was fighting against them. How could anything be more demoralizing? But isn't this what we do to each other when we do not support each other in the war against the evil one? To face this battle alone is to invite discouragement . . . or even disaster. In this mortal combat against the evil one, we must all find our place in the team's mission! Deep inside, we long to find our singular fit in a larger cause. Many people strive to find purpose in the work-a-day world. But this world is temporary, at best. It is futile to make a career or possessions in this world our ultimate end goal, no matter how successful these may be. Such pursuits will not last, nor will they be fulfilling. And, as Ecclesiastes 3:11 reminds us, God "*has placed eternity in our hearts.*" We want the long game. We want fulfillment that will last. No matter how successful our career, how large our house, how huge our bank account, or how extensive our social media platform, these simply will not suffice. As the writer of Ecclesiastes repeatedly reminds us, such undertakings, apart from God's greater purpose, are "vanity, all vanity."

Nope, our young disciples need to find something far more fulfilling if we want them to experience a satisfying life. Where may such satisfaction be found? You may be shocked to hear this, but it may be found at Church.

See? I knew you would be shocked. And so would millions of other faithful churchgoers who sit like automatons in church, passively occupying their pews week after week. We were meant to thrive in the fellowship of the Body, as the believers did in Acts 2. We need a place to belong, a greater purpose, and people to serve with, knowing that others have our back. Philippians 2:4 says, "*Let each of you look not only to his own interests, but also to the interests of others.*"

191

Perhaps the problem is that we simply do not understand why we even gather at the church house. We may think it is to sit and watch others perform, teach, sing, etc. But there is *so* much more. Encouraging and serving is not about making the Church comfortable inside but making us courageous for the battle outside. And we will all need plenty of Encouraging for that!

Chick-fil-A founder Truett Cathy quipped, "The way you can tell someone needs encouragement is if they are breathing."[23] What, then, do we really mean by "Encouraging" each other? How will we "instill courage" in our young disciples to complete our mission before His return? This will be an inside job. Our task with our disciples—to engage them with the Body—is not only important but imperative! To carry out the Great Commission, they need a Great Community.

Serving others is God's pathway to fulfillment! Not getting but giving. What a concept. Didn't Paul remind us in Acts 20:35 that Jesus said it is more blessed to give than to receive? Engaging your disciples to serve others in lowly positions is a critical factor in their spiritual development. I led some teenagers several years ago to repair the roof of a poor elderly lady's house. She came out of her house with tea and cake that she could not afford to give. She wept as she hugged each of us. One of my students said later, "I have always thought I wasn't worth anything, that I didn't matter to anyone. But I mattered to her." We don't appreciate our worth until we give ourselves away. Has it occurred to us that it is the janitor who has the most keys? He can access any room in a mansion! Why? Because he serves. Guiding your disciples to serve within the Body is not just a good idea. Serving others gives them access to great fulfillment in life.

SERVING WAS MODELED BY JESUS

Before His arrest and crucifixion, Jesus washed His disciples' feet. He stooped before them rather than speaking from a lofty podium. They didn't see this coming. They protested, refusing at first to allow it. Then Jesus explained, *"Do you know what I have done for you? You call me Teacher and Lord—and you are speaking rightly, since that is what I am. So if I, your Lord and Teacher have washed your feet, you also ought to wash one another's feet. For I have given you an example, that you also should do just as I have done for you. Truly I tell you, a servant is not greater than his master, and a messenger is not greater than the one who sent him. If you know these things, you are blessed if you do them"* (John 13:12–17). The disciples would soon become Apostles, spiritual fathers. But that lofty station began with Jesus' lowly service.

In the youth group, we chose to start disciples' service by giving them menial tasks. In fact, we celebrated that "lowly" role. Jesus said, *"For even the Son of Man did not come to be served, but to serve, and to give his life as a ransom for many"* (Mark 10:45). When we present discipleship opportunities to our students, we remind them, "You are here to help get underneath this group and lift up everyone in the group above yourselves."

Jeff, a senior, came to me to ask for more ministry opportunities. He was already leading one of our largest student-led home clubs and was the star quarterback for his high school football team. Are you kidding me, Jeff? So, I gave him a group of middle school boys to shepherd. Guess what? Those boys' world started on youth group nights when Jeff came through the door, hair slicked back from a shower after football workouts. It seemed that their goal in life was to bring Jeff to the floor in a wrestling match. Chairs would sometimes fly through the air as those little guys tackled him, hanging around his neck, his arms, and both legs. They couldn't seem to bring him down. Instead, Jeff would carry them around the room, sometimes on his shoulders. Now, that was my picture of servanthood. Even now, I can picture the look on those boys' faces as they paraded around the youth room on his shoulders. Perched up there, they were like the king of the world! He was lifting them up from the bottom, high above himself, the picture of serving.

The key to servant leadership is to realize that servants get underneath the whole group to boost them up. Of course, students' opportunities should increase over time. This is the way it is with any sport, right? You start out in the minors, but you hope to eventually make it to the major leagues. Jesus found common fishermen and painted them a picture. It was a picture of greatness. But that greatness would necessarily begin at the bottom. Underneath everyone else.

SERVING INSTILLS HUMILITY

We are all familiar with the "love chapter" in 1 Corinthians 13. However, the context for that chapter was the problems occurring in that fellowship due to pride. The gifts, explained in 1 Corinthians 12, were designed to bless the Church, not to boast about personal abilities.

How are we to help our young disciples to discover their true value to the fellowship? By giving them grunt jobs. Uh-huh. I knew you would love that. The best leaders are often those who have first served in lowly servant roles and unexalted positions. People who have worked at low-paying jobs before becoming leaders really know what it means to be at the bottom of the barrel. Jesus knew about being at the bottom. He began His earthly ministry in a smelly manger.

How many of us have had leaders who think they know everything about a task but have never actually performed that task? But one thing is sure; those people who rise from lowly positions tend to remember what it was like to be at the bottom. Service develops the character of Christ.

At the Global Institute, our interns begin by mastering small tasks. Our staff members accompany the interns to perform menial jobs, teaching what they know about the task as they work side by side. Hopefully, our interns know that we would not ask them to do something that we do not practice or would not be willing to do ourselves.

There is a standing joke among our interns about weed eaters (we call them weed whackers at Global because we don't eat weeds, we whack them). We live on a mountain, and we must take care of the slopes lest the view disappear when little saplings spring up and become trees that block the amazing views. I, along with everyone on campus, have tackled those slopes to whack those weeds. I have personally weed whacked in several countries as part of mission team projects. I jokingly formed an "International Christian Weed Whackers Association." Some of my interns aim to join it as they weed whack in multiple countries where we minister. Their can-do spirit fills me with joy as they learn to tackle menial tasks with gusto. On one trip, Laura (an intern) quickly started weed whacking before I could get my weed whacker running. She was so proud to be the first of us to weed whack in that country. We still laugh about that.

Serving Instills Appreciation for Others' Contributions

Every disciple should have had enough experience with menial tasks to at least appreciate the effort that others put into them. And they will more quickly rise to the defense and praise of those who fulfill these menial tasks in the future.

Grunt work is good work. Put your teen disciples to work setting up chairs. They can serve on the greeting team. They can help set up audio equipment or clean up after youth services. They can help assemble and organize game items. Young disciples can begin to serve by helping to prepare, bring, or serve refreshments at the group meetings. Computer enthusiasts can help with social media tasks or work in the tech booth. They can be prayer board keepers. There is no end to the possibilities. Later, they can move from preparing for activities to executing them. Eventually, they will step into even greater spiritual leadership roles to lead in small groups, worship, teaching, and more. As students serve in menial tasks, they learn the value of small things. They value the work of people who work behind the scenes to enable greater things.

Serving Instills the Value of Teamwork

Part of the discipling task is to help young disciples to learn that they are part of a greater mission. Our young disciples accept serving roles as we guide them toward the Ability (leadership) level. Every disciple is placed on a "servant team."

Young disciples learn through participation in these teams that everyone has a place on the team, and everyone is needed to achieve the mission. As they spend time together with other disciple teammates to accomplish a common task, they begin to learn to value the support of others.

It is often difficult for leaders to relinquish tasks to their discipleship students. It may be easier to do things yourself to ensure that tasks will be done right. But when students take charge, they get more involved. They listen and work together more intently with their teammates. Also, you can hold students more accountable for growth when they accept responsibility. Why so? Because they are allowed to experience genuine ownership. They also discover how their service inside the Church supports their mission outside the Church. As they are led to engage in Evangelism, they will recognize the value of support by the Body to accomplish its larger mission.

SERVING IS THE GATEWAY TO GREATER THINGS

When students are empowered to invest in ministry, they will remain involved, hopefully for the rest of their lives. Teens often leap to the challenge when given meaningful opportunities to try new skills in a positive environment. When adults do it all, students fold their hands. But watch what happens when teens are asked to become part of the team. Those clasped hands become clammy! Hearts race. This is way more fun! Without responsibility, there is no opportunity for achievement, a basic human need. Serving becomes a pathway to discover their greater purpose.

We call our teams "servant teams" rather than "leadership teams" for a reason. Jesus said that those who would be leaders must first become like Him, the servant of all (Mark 10:45). Before they are ready to move into leadership roles at the Ability stage of growth, our disciples must first learn to serve. Later, as they demonstrate consistency, we step up responsibilities for the older students to learn leadership at the Ability stage. Leadership must be earned.

The key is that there is always more! Greater opportunities lie ahead for those who serve faithfully. We must provide a pathway for our young disciples to learn competencies for effective living in all areas of life. As they acquire more skills, they become more valuable. At the Ability stage they will provide a role model for others to follow. Doug Franklin, founder of LeaderTreks, told me that he thinks of discipleship as the bullpen for future leaders. I like that; we should always be "warming up" the next pitchers and players to put in the game!

Serving Instills the Value of Personal Fulfillment

In his book, *Understanding People*, Dr. Larry Crabb said, "We experience this desire for impact in many ways. Inspecting a newly waxed car or a freshly cut lawn provides a measure of legitimate satisfaction: 'I did it. Because I expended energy, things look better. I made a difference.'" Crabb defined the thirst for impact as "a desire to be adequate for a meaningful task, a desire to know that we are capable of taking hold of our world and doing something valuable and well."[24] Our goal as disciplers is that young people become fully engaged with the Body of Christ to accomplish the epic mission He set before us. Now, that is fulfilling!

Serving is the Pathway to Gift Discovery

The Accountability level of personal spiritual growth should enable teens to discover their spiritual giftedness. Giftedness? Is that really a thing for teenagers? You bet it is! As they work together in various teams, they begin to recognize unique ways that their contributions make a supernatural impact in the larger mission. Serving becomes the pathway to a lifetime of fulfillment as they discover and practice their gifts in the Body. We will tackle that amazing topic in the next chapter. In the meantime, while believers are finding their spiritual gifts, they are certainly finding meaning within the Body through service.

A Word to the Wise

In any case, your disciples must learn to serve. They need to realize that sometimes it is just about jumping in there with fellow saints to get the job done. During this Accountability phase in young disciples' growth, we guide them to develop the attitude of servanthood. It may not be easy, especially in an entitlement culture. But those who learn these qualities often rise up as great and godly leaders in the future. Faithfulness in small things will lead to greater things.

At camp one summer, a young man with a guitar wowed everyone with his musical expertise during a variety show. He was very talented. And charismatic. Later, the youth minister from his church came to me. "What did you think of the guitarist who sang at the variety show?" I responded, "Wow, he was very talented. Is he from your church?"

"Oh, yes. Well, he is not a member yet. I'm thinking of putting him on our praise team." I asked if the young man was a believer. "Oh, not yet. He probably will be soon, though. I think if we get him involved in the band, he will come to Christ."

What would you say to the youth pastor? I hesitated—but only for a brief second—before plunging in: "I wouldn't advise putting a non-believer in a leadership role on a stage, regardless of his talent. If you do this, you may signal to all your youth group that you value talent above faith, skill over service, and charisma over character. Beyond that, he may wrongly perceive that faith is little more than an act on a stage, about getting attention rather than giving service. You might give him a task, but not on the stage in the beginning. Let him help set up chairs in the youth room for a while. Help him become a believer in his own time. Then disciple him for a while before giving him leadership responsibility." The youth leader didn't listen.

The next year the youth group returned to camp. I noticed that the young man was not with the group, so I inquired about him. I almost wish I hadn't. The youth leader sheepishly told me that he had put the young man on stage with the band. He later got a worship team vocalist pregnant, and both had dropped out of church. Oh, my. I had no words. My heart sank through the floor.

Leadership must be earned. Don't rush the learning curve with your disciples. Use discipleship as an opportunity for students to pick up lifelong character traits by serving others. That will help seal their own intrinsic value as well as the value of those they serve at work, at home, and at church. Suffice it to say, we believe that character precedes competencies. We prize their reputation as humble and trustworthy servants at home, in the world, and in the workplace. Give your students a lasting gift, one that will keep on giving. Train them to be competent servants.

CHAPTER 13

SERVANT TEAMS: MOVING INTO SPIRITUAL GIFTS

How to Help Disciples Engage in Lifelong Service

We all hope that youth group members will remain fully and faithfully engaged in the life and work of the Church as adults. But statistics don't lie. Students are graduating and leaving the Church in droves. If students are to find their place in the Body, then our discipleship must help them find ways to serve that will last beyond the youth group.

As stated in Ephesians 4:12, we Equip young disciples to take personal responsibility for spiritual self-discipline. Then, we lead them into Evangelistic sharing. But beyond that, a young disciple should also learn how he or she uniquely fits within the Body to help bear others' burdens as a fully functioning team member. This Encouraging task points to spiritual gifts.

If Accountability only involves learning to take care of oneself, something is missing. We must learn to take responsibility for ourselves so we may function as part of the larger team effort.

Otherwise, we would become more of a burden upon the Church than a blessing to the Church.

I grew up in a town where Sunday church attendance was expected. My family had a Saturday night routine: we read the Sunday school lesson, memorized the memory verse, filled out the offering envelope (with tithe inside), and polished our shoes. All of those tasks, including shoe-shining, were religious activities, you see—at least it seemed so to me. I wasn't responsible for what happened at church; I only had to be there, ready to receive. The rest was up to someone else. Some churchgoers get stuck in that mentality for their whole lives.

In some youth ministries the youth have little or no responsibility for their program. Their job is to show up. They don't bring their Bibles to Bible study, much less study their Bible on their own. They attend and lean back with folded arms and wait for the leaders to do it all. If the event goes well, the leaders get credit for it. If things go poorly, the leaders get criticism for it. The students have been conditioned to sit there passively and not interrupt the leader's program.

In many churches, the Body seems passive, dazed, and disorganized. It relies upon its pastors and officers to conduct the church's mission, from Equipping to Evangelizing to Encouraging. That was definitely not the plan outlined in Ephesians 4:11–13! Can you imagine how pleased the Devil must be with this arrangement? Ninety percent or more of the Body is being carried on the shoulders of a very tired and stretched ten percent who are called ministers, pastors, and elders. The rest of the church is nearly spiritually comatose. Satan is left with only a few people to target, the ones holding up the rest of the congregation. How convenient for him. He only needs to knock the legs out from under the servant leaders, and perhaps the whole congregation will come tumbling down.

One church where I served offered me a tenth-year sabbatical from my youth ministry duties to conduct some research on other youth ministries around the country. I chose to visit several churches on the west coast. Many of these churches were very well known across the United States. One Sunday, I attended a megachurch and visited the youth service. I was stunned at what I witnessed. The youth minister gave the welcome. The youth minister led the music, playing a guitar. The youth minister led the Bible study. The youth minister prayed a closing prayer. The youth minister was amazing.

There were perhaps a dozen other adults in the room with nearly 250 students. But with seven thousand people on the church campus that morning, I had expected at least seven hundred to one thousand students on the premises. The reason there weren't that many might have been partly due to the weight the youth minister carried. He was trying to do everything by himself.

There must be a better way. People become more invested where they are more involved! The need in many—if not most—churches is not for more paid staff members. Rather, the need is for all members to work together, serving in their spiritual giftedness. Attending Sunday services does not meet this need. But this reality would appear to be a mystery to many teens and adults. Serving is neither emphasized nor practiced effectively in many churches. There is a better way for your young people, a way that will lead them to find amazing fulfillment. The pathway to that fulfillment is in helping students to discover their spiritual gifts.

FIND A PATHWAY FOR DISCIPLES TO SERVE THE CHURCH

How do we begin to wean students from sitting to serving? How do we help them to find their giftedness? Here's a possible pathway: start by developing intentional service opportunities right within your youth ministry. But how, you may ask? Good question. For me, it was a journey. I had to work my way through several models of student participation in youth ministry. I have experienced—even led—youth ministry using each of these models described next.

Model #1: Youth Leader Alone

In many places this would be the standard approach to youth ministry: secure a leader and let that leader do it all. That was my gig at my first church. And it was a blast. We grew from three teens on the first night to over sixty in short order. But as the youth group grew, my charisma seemed to shrink. I just could not get around to relate to everyone as I had in the beginning months. Eventually, we topped out. At the time I thought we were doing great. But looking back, I realize that it would have been far better if other leaders had been empowered to help minister with the teens. They attended faithfully, but it never occurred to me to help them discover their gifts. And the teens? It could have been so much more productive had I understood the value of discipling future leaders. Sorry, everyone. Helping people find their gifts had not hit my grid.

Model #2: Youth Leader and Youth Committee—Ministry for Youth

In this model, the adults develop and lead ministry activities, events, and programs for the youth. This is ministry *for* youth; teenagers are the recipients but provide no planning or leadership. Instead, the adults in the congregation assume all the responsibility for youth work. In this youth committee approach, the students have no stake in the ministry's success or failure. This was the model that my first full-time church, Calvary, had employed since the1950's. The church was blessed with adults who had been working with the youth for decades. There was a well-developed calendar of activities in place when I arrived. The committee, comprised only of adults, made all the plans, organized all the events, and provided on-site supervision. It seemed to work. So many adults involved? Great!

However, a problem quickly became apparent: The youth were passive. They were content with the many programs designed to keep them involved, but they had little to no sense of ownership. This was someone else's program, not theirs. They were free to show up—or not—based on whatever else might appeal to them at any given moment.

The result of this model? The youth ministry did not grow beyond the youth whose families attended the church. For several months we had no newcomers. None. The youth group was not only in-grown, but it was also more than content to remain that way. We were not even thinking about reaching out beyond the church youth to involve other students. It was almost like a church nursery, a holding tank for spiritual infants. Its function was to babysit the kids and keep them entertained and out of trouble. The objective was to protect the youth rather than to prepare them to live and lead effectively in the future.

It didn't work. They were neither engaged nor staying out of trouble. I had no idea what to do with this. I understood the problem, but I struggled to find a solution. God was allowing me to see the need for something more. But the critical nature of engaging students in either serving or giftedness was still not clear to me. This was a work in progress.

Model #3: Youth Council— Ministry with Youth (for Themselves)

I stumbled upon a third model of youth ministry while serving in my next church, Maywood, where there was a youth council. Different from a youth committee, this group was composed of adults *and* youth who planned events together for the youth ministry. However, the planning was limited to activities designed for the youth who already attended. The focus was mostly on planning special events like fun trips, retreats, camps, etc. But it was a step up from the adult-only youth committee model. At least a few young people were involved and had some responsibility for ministry events. Still, teen involvement in planning was usually limited to only those few young people along with parents and other adults. The youth council met only once a month or so. It was better; more people were involved. But something wasn't quite right.

Model #4: Servant Teams—Ministry by Youth (for Others)

While I was at Trinity in San Antonio, I began to experiment with a different approach. I invited our young disciples to take an active part not only in special event planning but also to assist with the regular weekly programming. The activities they planned were not just for them, but *by* them *for* others. The number of teen participants began to multiply as these young disciples grasped that they were truly needed and valued.

In this servant team approach, our discipleship teens were enlisted to assist in a variety of ways to develop ownership in their youth ministry. More importantly, the teens' involvement in ministry was designed to point them to their spiritual giftedness, not just for youth ministry in the present but for the congregation long after they graduated from school.

This may be a path you would want to explore for your disciples. We experimented with this and made incremental changes over time. The requirements we initially placed on disciples in their servant teams were far less strenuous in the early years than they became later. We found that as the demand to be part of the teams increased, so did the standards. It was amazing to see how willing those young people were to rise to the increasing requirements.

Here's the irony. Chris Wilterdink, director of Young People's Ministries Program Development at Discipleship Ministries, said it this way: "It may seem backward, but in order to increase the amount of participation from youth, we need to ask more of them."[25] The key is to up your game, *not* to make discipleship seem easy! We invite our young disciples to roll up their sleeves to serve. Then, in the midst of serving, students are able to discover their spiritual gifts.

FOCUS YOUR DISCIPLES NOW FOR FUTURE SERVICE

Jesus told His disciples at the last supper that the Spirit would come to empower them to serve Him. Within the Body, as Paul writes in Galatians 6:2, we *"bear one another's burdens, and so fulfill the law of Christ."* Every believer is empowered to fulfill a vital role.

But in many churches, this is not happening.

I have seen this up close. After agreeing to serve as an interim for a large church, I walked into the midweek youth service for the first time. There were perhaps 150 students sitting in the old sanctuary where the youth met after the church had built a new one. As soon as I walked in, I could see the clear divisions. On my left were the middle schoolers, lots of them; they were a beehive of activity. To my right were the ninth through eleventh graders. In the far back, on the last pew next to the exit, sat the twelfth graders. They were mostly quiet, many with arms folded.

They didn't need words to speak loudly to me and to the whole group. These seniors were telling everyone that they were out, or at least as close to the exit as possible. There was an air that perhaps they were insulted at being in the same room with middle schoolers. They didn't like being treated the same way now as they were when they entered the youth group six years ago.

Unfortunately, too many older students in our youth groups are biding time to move on, graduate, get out. They are bored, sitting as close to the exit as possible, waiting for the bell.

In fact, some of them look ahead at the students who graduated before them and have gone on to college. Most of those students aren't even involved in church anymore. Older high school students are keenly aware of this. They may wonder, "If I am going to drop out of church in any case when I graduate from high school, why shouldn't I just go ahead and drop out right now? There is no challenge here anyway. I could be using my time better elsewhere."

This attitude is a sure indication that the youth group is not being *prepared* for life but merely *protected* from it. Older students might even wonder, "Prepare? For what? What is there here to prepare for? More sitting? When we graduate, if we even remain in the church, we will just sit in pews to endure adult programs, which sounds really awkward and boring." E-yikes!

FULFILL DISCIPLES' COMMISSION THROUGH SPIRITUAL GIFTS

Youth ministry should be preparing young disciples for lifelong service in the Body of Christ by leading young people to explore their giftedness and to employ their gifts to strengthen the Church for its grand and eternal mission. You know . . . the Great Commission.

But in many youth groups, this goal doesn't occur to the teens . . . or to their leaders. How sad it is to realize that so many talented and energetic young people will graduate from the youth group believing that Church is where others do something *for* them, but that the Church's vital mission is certainly not *by* them. That is, if they even decide to stick around to participate at all.

Whether you are the youth minister or serve as a youth discipler, you should seek to give your students something to do in church. Something that matters and will enable them to explore their value to God by accessing His power, His gifts. Something that has eternal impact.

In any military unit, special tasks and skills are required for the unit to function properly. Similarly, spiritual gifts are assigned to believers by God (Romans 12:3) and are for the good of the Body. The New Testament tells us that He distributes special abilities—

let's call them supernatural abilities—to "edify" (the word we use with teens is Encourage) the Body of Christ. These are the distinct spiritual gifts listed in passages like 1 Corinthians 12, Ephesians 4, 1 Peter 4, and Romans 12:6-8 where Paul writes, *"We have different gifts, according to the grace given to each of us. If your gift is prophesying, then prophesy in accordance with your faith; if it is serving, then serve; if it is teaching, then teach; if it is to encourage, then give encouragement; if it is giving, then give generously; if it is to lead, do it diligently; if it is to show mercy, do it cheerfully."* You might wonder why we should even deal with spiritual gifts as we disciple teens. In truth, this should be a priority in our discipleship for at least two reasons.

Reason #1: Servants' Competence

When young people discover and exercise their individual spiritual gifts, they find a sense of fulfillment that is hard to describe. Operating within one's gifts cannot be compared to talent or skill sets. There is a palpable difference between spiritual gifts and natural abilities or skills.

Let's suppose that two musicians sing worship solos for the congregation. The first is a skilled and well-trained vocalist. She has been educated in music at the university and has a degree in music arts. She sings a spiritual song to the congregation, and the worshipers are amazed at her craft. Her vocal range and control over her breathing are quite amazing. She hits every note precisely. After she finishes, the worshipers applaud enthusiastically.

Then a second soloist stands to sing. She is neither educated musically nor poised in her presentation. But as soon as she opens her mouth to sing, the audience leans in. You can sense the presence of God in the room as a hush falls over the congregation. After the last note falls from her lips, there is a moment of silence while the church takes in what has just happened. Then applause breaks out, slowly at first and then more vigorously as the audience starts to stand to their feet. You can see tears falling on the cheeks of many. God has entered the room. The congregation is fully aware that this moment is a "God moment."

What was the difference? The first soloist sang with professional excellence. We enjoyed it. The second soloist employed the gift of exhortation, and God spoke through her as she sang to bless the people, instilling courage in them to tackle their mission beyond the church doors.

That soloist will sense the power of the Holy Spirit moving through her as she sings. She is bringing a convicting message to the Body. She will know it has happened. She will know that it was not her but the Spirit that did the work through her. The Spirit moves through believers just as wind flows through a flute to bring beautiful music to listeners. If giftedness is not about the Spirit's breath moving into and then through us to build up others, then what is it about?

When we operate within our spiritual giftedness, we feel an amazing exhilaration and sense of purposefulness and fulfillment that can hardly be explained. When our disciple students begin to operate within their spiritual gifts, they become more fully alive as they sense the Spirit moving through them to bless other believers. Those disciples will know beyond doubt that the Lord has used their lives to display His power through the gifts He bestowed. They feel the wind of His Spirit alive and moving through them. The Spirit's moving deep within them is how they know they are truly alive! How fulfilling to know the Spirit is moving and working through us.

Reason #2: Saints' Courage

There is a corollary and even more profound benefit to operating within our giftedness. Yes, our disciples find fulfillment in the Body when they employ their gifts. But the greater purpose of gifts is to focus the congregation on God's presence and to empower them for His purpose. 1 Peter 4:10 says, *"Each of you should use whatever gift you have received to serve others, as faithful stewards of God's grace in its various forms."* Everyone has at least one gift to serve the Body. As your disciples discover and use their gifts, people are truly Encouraged (instilled with courage). God's power is released in the body like a surge of adrenaline coursing through it to prepare it for the battle that awaits just outside the building.

This operation of the Spirit cannot be matched, cloned, copied, or artificially reproduced. The gifts do not merely entertain us but Encourage us. The gifts are strictly business—Church business. One way a student knows his gifts are being used is that people will let him know!

Although spiritual gifts are employed to benefit the Body, they are not designed merely for the congregation to be blessed. Rather, gifts are employed to prepare the Body to *be* a blessing to a waiting world. Gifts enable us to carry out the mission Jesus placed before us.

This function is completely unique to the people of God. His gifts alone will accomplish the objective of Encouraging and strengthening the Body of Christ for its mission in the world.

Lead Young Disciples to Discover Their Gifts

I have had the great joy of seeing high schoolers become so fulfilled using their gifts in youth ministry that they continue to assist in leadership roles long after they graduate.

Some of my students have even chosen to continue their education online or at a local college rather than go away to college so that they could continue ministering in our church. Now, that is really saying something, considering that so many students are eager to "get outta' town and away from home." Even some former high school grads who left for college returned every summer to volunteer with the college-aged summer staff as team leaders for the summer youth program and youth camp. Why do they desire to connect? It has something to do with their fulfillment during their high school years as they battled the evil one to reach lost souls and found their place in the King's battalion by using their gifts.

As a discipler, your encouragement, admonishment, and exhortation will have a profound impact on your disciples. One semester, a very fine young man who graduated and went to Baylor University wrote me a letter. In that letter, he said some very nice things about what he had learned as a high school student while he was discipled at Trinity Church. Then he wrote that it was imperative that he see me personally when he returned home for Thanksgiving. I could not imagine what he wanted to talk about. I feared that something was wrong at school or home.

But when we talked on a Friday night, he said, "Roger, I know this is probably very forward of me, and I am embarrassed to ask, but I feel a deep conviction to come home for a year and work with the youth at Trinity as an intern. I know there are extremely

213

high standards for working with our young people, and I feel very unworthy, but would you at least pray about it?"

We were sitting on the curb in the church's parking lot. In the gathering darkness I just silently praised God. Chris was a wonderful young man who was deeply committed to Christ. I was glad it was dark outside because I started to tear up. I thought to myself, "It is I who should feel unworthy to be a part of a ministry where such a young man as this would want to serve."

And then I thought back to Chris' rise to leadership among our students. In those moments I was reminded that Encouraging truly played a big role in this young man's growth. I couldn't help but think of the times when Chris had been Encouraged publicly and privately by his fellow youth and by the college students who discipled him and served with him. I am certain that God used both the public response and the private feedback to shape and mold Chris into the fine leader that he was! He used his gifts to serve others. As he did, his life had an impact.

So many young people have great difficulty in accepting the idea that they truly *belong* somewhere, that they are needed and valued. That is a big miss for the whole Church.

Gifts—Nice or Necessary?

The Holy Spirit Himself is God's gift to His children. But the Spirit also brings gifts for us to unwrap and put to good use. I hope we have made at least enough noise about disciples serving in the Body and learning their spiritual giftedness that it has hit your radar, youth discipler! Helping your young disciples to engage intentionally in the life of the Church by discovering and practicing their unique spiritual gifts is not just a nicety. It is more like a necessity.

The hard test of whether we have been able to reach this objective may not become apparent until *after* they have graduated from high school. It is then that we will really know whether they have found the sort of service within the Church that will produce in them the appetite to remain there, fully engaged for a lifetime.

PART SIX

SETTING THE STAGE

Graduating into Spiritual Ability

CHAPTER 14

LAUNCH DATE

*How to Evaluate Whether a Disciple
Is Ready for the Ability Stage*

As we approach the end of our journey exploring discipleship with teens at the middle Accountability stage, let's review the end goal. What does a fully functioning disciple look like? When do we know that a student has successfully moved through Accountability and is truly poised for the final Ability level as a spiritual leader? High school graduations should indicate that students are ready for the next stage of life. In the spiritual realm, when are students ready to launch into servant leadership, the Ability stage?

These are important questions and worthy of consideration. If indeed we are attempting to prepare spiritual children to become fully functioning adults, we should be aware of the marks of spiritual maturity.

Jesus led His disciples through three years of daily training. He knew that He had only so much time with them as He "*set his face toward Jerusalem*" (Luke 9:51). He was on a mission. When

His moment finally arrived, He knew it would be commencement time for His disciples.

If you have been through graduation ceremonies, you know how these things go. There is probably a lot of drama, usually a family gathering, hopefully with a big meal. There may be gifts and probably a VIP talking to us about our future. It is a big deal.

In John 13:1–17, there was a graduation ceremony for the disciples. Jesus knew His hour had come to depart. He was passing the baton to the disciples. The ceremony included a meal, an address about the future by a celebrity, and yes, gifts. Or at least the promise of a gift—the coming of the Holy Spirit.

But . . . it would not appear that His disciples were ready, based on what happened next. By all accounts they failed. Instead of stepping up to stand strong for their Master, they fled. Rather than face the Pharisees, one even assisted in the plot to arrest Jesus. Carry on with the mission? Nah. Even after Jesus appeared to the disciples following His Resurrection, Thomas refused to believe "unless" and "until." Huh?

Which part of this looks like success?

Jesus left His disciples to carry on, to lead fellow believers into the future of the Church. But they left Him, running for cover when the soldiers came to arrest Him in the Garden of Gethsemane. Instead of moving forward, they ran back! Back to their lives before Him.

Apparently, Jesus knew something about His followers that was not apparent to anyone else. The observing world would have declared the whole discipling enterprise of Jesus a disaster. At that point in time, even the disciples themselves saw it all as a devastating failure.

When the disciples fled, they hid out in an upper room. In fact, some even went back to their hometown to take up fishing again. It seemed they were done. The truth is, if the Holy Spirit—the presence of Jesus Himself—had not arrived in that upper room in Acts 2, and then into their hearts, the odds were definitely against those disciples.

Jesus knew. He knew they would overcome. He knew they would conquer. They would find their wings and fly. The Resurrection confounded them. The upper room confined them. But the coming of the Spirit changed them forever. Everything that we have been talking about in this book boils down to one thing: a disciple must surrender everything to Jesus, learning to obediently follow the leadership of His Spirit daily in ways that are obvious to all.

How do you know your disciple is ready to graduate to the next level, that of the "spiritual father" (Ability stage)? Like Jesus, you can also know. It's not that hard, really. Let's go back to our definition of youth discipleship given in Chapter Three:

"A disciple is one who is surrendering to the Spirit
and accountable to a more mature saint to develop
self disciplined character, Scriptural confidence, and servant leader competence,
in order to engage in disciple making."

Wouldn't a graduate be one who has consistently demonstrated these qualities in daily life? Perhaps we could state this definition of discipleship more from an outcome standpoint:

> *"A disciple grad is one who consistently surrenders to the Spirit, demonstrating self-disciplined <u>character</u>, Scriptural <u>confidence</u>, servant leader <u>competence</u>, and readiness to become a disciple-maker."*

Notice that I left out the words, "is accountable to a more mature believer." This does not mean that your disciple grads are no longer accountable to anyone for their personal spiritual life or actions. But they have been weaned from dependence on others and are standing strong by God's Spirit to serve Christ with self-discipline. A grad-ready disciple is one who has been a good follower and is now ready to step into leadership.

From that post-discipleship perspective of the definition, let's attempt to pull together a summary of our journey through this book to describe a grad-ready disciple. Short version: a disciple is one who has learned to follow Jesus consistently. As he is Equipped in a personal relationship with Jesus, he is led by the Spirit to begin sharing God's love with a lost world held hostage by Satan (Evangelism). And he is using his spiritual gifts to minister as a teammate with other believers (Encouraging). But let's delve deeper into this for a few moments. Can we study your disciples, the ones you have been working with for a while now? Let's see who they love, where they go, what they do. How do we discern that they are ready to launch?

DISCIPLE GRADS EXEMPLIFY SELF-DISCIPLINED CHARACTER

God's first and foremost commandment is the Great Commandment, to love Him fully and completely, Mark 12:30. This is how we begin to reflect His glory into His creation. God used words like "subdue" and "rule" in Genesis 1:28 to describe our role on earth. Guided by the Spirit, we restore God's glory to reflect His creativity and orderliness. But all that starts by submitting to God in subduing ourselves through eager self-discipline. Only as our young disciples demonstrate this quality will they become ready to serve others. 1 Timothy 3:2-3 tells us that a disciple who rises to the Ability stage must be ". . . *above reproach, faithful to his wife, temperate, self-controlled, respectable, hospitable, able to teach, not given to drunkenness, not violent but gentle, not quarrelsome, not a lover of money.*" Clearly, self-discipline is our proper spiritual response to Christ and a chief characteristic of one who rises to the Ability stage.

1. Graduates Exhibit Intellectual Self-Discipline.

Our young disciples have come a long way when they use critical thinking to seek and identify facts and can discern the difference between light and dark, good and evil, truth and lies. Like the writer of Proverbs, they seek to put facts together to make wise, godly decisions that are based on God's Truth. Their decisions consider both the present situation and the impact of their decisions on other people and future situations. They continue to be humble and teachable. They guard their schedule and control their spending habits, keeping long-term goals in view.

2. Graduates Demonstrate Physical Self-Discipline

People who have developed discipline in this area express this from the inside out. As Paul said in 1 Corinthians 3:16, they treat their own bodies as the temple of the Holy Spirit. Whatever they eat or drink is taken with awareness that God is the owner of their bodies, and He is jealous for what He owns. They regulate their diet, exercise and rest. Beyond their internal health, these young people adorn their bodies, not to call attention to themselves but to honor God.

As ambassadors (2 Corinthians 5:20), grads take care of their surroundings to the extent possible. They do not depend on others to deal with messes; they tackle these themselves and enlist others to assist. They make up their beds and help out around the house. But that is only the beginning of their awareness of their environment.

Using Paul's example in Philippians 4:11, grads have learned to be content. They have brought their physical and consumer appetites and urges under control. Things that once drew them into sin may test them but no longer control them. They do not steal or cheat, and they are not selfish or greedy. Their hearts break over their sin and the sins of others.

These students care about their world as a sacred trust. They take an interest in the environment and try to do their part. They are aware of the impact of their choices, purchases, and decisions upon the environment and their witness. But they do not treat the environment as if it is the only thing. They realize that there is a still greater environment, the kingdom in which God reigns and sin is defeated. Their home is not earth, but Heaven.

3. Graduates Practice Social Self-Discipline

Character shows up in graduates who maturely and compassionately relate to other people. Just as God is relational, they value friendships, trustworthiness, and godly loyalty.

Still, these disciples look to God for His approval and their identity rather than to seek that from other people. This frees them to be themselves and to value other people as God's creations.

Relationships are important to them, but they are not enslaved to others' opinions. Their godly self-worth can withstand both criticism and compliments. And they are able to find greater delight in the success of others.

As commanded in Ephesians 5:4, coarse talk that may have once amused them is no longer amusing. They mourn the godless lifestyles they see abounding in our culture that are celebrated in the tabloids, the movies, and the social media. They exhibit unusual restraint in the use of social media. They are able to self-monitor their own speech, speaking truth in love. Knowing that all humans are broken and imperfect, they can be honest without being judgmental.

In fact, disciple grads have gained the ability to deal with conflict in a God-honoring manner with a view to resolve differences and maintain peace wherever possible. They seek win-win solutions.

4. Graduates Continue in Spiritual Self-Discipline

We will expand on this in the paragraphs below on Scriptural confidence. Suffice it to say here, disciples have owned their relationship with God, submitting to Him in all things. They respect human authority but look to His Word as the final authority. They continue to be humble and teachable but do not remain dependent upon spiritual elders to take care of their relationship with God. Their spiritual intake is regular, consistent, and unprompted. It is pouring out in their attitude, their posture, their speech, pretty much every aspect of their lives. They understand that God has set boundaries and limitations for them and have found freedom in that reality.

They have determined that those sins, habits, and vices that they once assumed were of little impact are actually burdens that weigh them down and lead to spiritual defeat.

DISCIPLE GRADS EXUDE SCRIPTURAL CONFIDENCE

We reviewed the process for teaching the Word in Chapter 9. In 1 John 2:12–14, John says a spiritual young man is not only strong in character, but also "*the word abides in him.*" We know disciples are ready for graduation when they are actively Equipping themselves in the Word. They are becoming confident, but that does not mean they are cocky. They have a spirit of humility, realizing that for everything they do know of Christ, there is so much more they do not know . . . yet. This reality only increases their appetite for the Word.

1. Graduates Constantly Read The Word

You will know that your disciples are ready to graduate when they feed themselves on their own. Not that they have no further need for others' teaching. No, no! In fact, they will be the ones in the group who always have pen in hand and the Bible open when the Word is taught. But they will not be like the child in the highchair, totally dependent upon others to feed them. They have an appetite for spiritual meat and go after it. Moreover, they have read through the Bible.

2. Graduates are Students of The Word

You will know your disciples are ready for the next stage when they have learned simple principles for Bible study, such as the inductive study method. They are studying on their own but are checking with you and others occasionally for clarification. They have a good study Bible and some solid study resources, and they know how to use them. They are doctrinally sound and steadily growing in their confidence in God's Word.

They will also have an appetite to start passing on what they have learned to others. What a refreshing moment it is when I sit under teaching by a young disciple of mine who has studied the Word for himself and is sharing its amazing veracity with others, making practical application of it to daily life. As a disciple studies the Word, it becomes evident that he desires not only to obey it, but also to share its truths and its stunning life-giving power with others.

3. Graduates are Memorizing The Word

It just goes without saying that disciples who are ready to graduate are continually memorizing portions of the Word. As the Psalmist said, Psalm 119:11, they are hiding God's Word in their hearts. Our disciple grads do not meet the opposition without continually strengthening their grip on the sword, the Word of God.

Unprompted by your pleading, your graduate-ready disciples are fully aware that they must regularly memorize Scripture. Thus, their Scriptural confidence comes from the inside out.

4. Graduates Meditate On and Pray According to The Word

Disciples who are ready to graduate into spiritual Ability are walking in the Spirit, praying often. They have demonstrated that they are not only knowledgeable in Scripture but also know how to apply Scripture to everyday life. They have developed solid decision-making skills that are based in God's Word.

After all, soon your grads will begin to disciple others. We want to know that they not only have the facts, but they are also able to guide their young followers into wise living, based on a strong Scriptural understanding. Just as the writer of the Proverbs highly prized the virtue of wisdom, your grads will desire to lead others to do the same.

Our hope is that those young disciples have learned to have a constant conversation with God by His Spirit and according to His Word. Their prayer life is ongoing, even beyond daily prayer times. As Paul admonished us to "*pray without ceasing*" (1 Thessalonians 5:17), they constantly seek the guidance of the Spirit through a robust prayer life. And as they pray, they often pray the very words of Scripture throughout their day. Walking in wisdom will require constant communicating in prayer with God's Spirit and connecting with God's Word. When needed, they fast for purity and preparation for battle.

5. Graduates Pray Constantly and likely Journal Their Journey

It should be your hope that your disciples pray unceasingly. They will probably also chronicle what they are learning from God's Spirit by His Word.

Friend, can you imagine what may come further down the road, when your own disciples share with others—not only spoken but also in written form—what God has taught them? Do you think you will be glad then that you helped them solidify the discipline of writing down what they have learned from the Spirit?

Many people of consequence throughout history have been writers and avid journalers. They recognized the importance of writing down their thoughts, and they understood the power of the written Word. When Johannes Gutenberg printed the first Bibles, he unleashed a firestorm. He knew. He recognized the power of words, both spoken and written. So should your disciples.

DISCIPLE GRADS EXPRESS SERVANT LEADER COMPETENCIES

1.Graduates Competently Engage with God's Great Commission (Evangelism)

Disciple grads are not only Scripturally confident but also competent in the spiritual battle. 1 John 2 tells us that a spiritual young man is one who does more than study the Word. He applies it, *"overcoming the evil one."* Head knowledge is not enough.

Many humans spend their lives searching for lost Eden. It is called by many names: nirvana, paradise, karma, etc. Some believe Heaven consists of whatever we can obtain on earth. Thus, they seek that elusive bliss in the finite world. Many have swallowed whole the Devil's lie that we can have Heaven on earth—our broken world—without God. Not your disciple grads. They know that it is God who put eternity in their hearts (Ecclesiastes 3:11), and they keep Heaven in view. They know that there is a better life, a more perfect world, and they act accordingly.

They experience the presence of Jesus who is with them by the Holy Spirit. He is the essence of Heaven, which is all about relationships . . . beginning with God and extending to fellow saints. Disciples know that the Holy Spirit is believers' downpayment, the foretaste of Heaven.

But for now, it is a war. Daily. Disciples arm themselves daily as admonished in Ephesians 6. Suited up with this spiritual armor, grads are realists who do not become mesmerized or distracted by the mirage of a Heaven here on earth. Max Lucado wrote, "Lower your expectations of earth. This isn't Heaven, so don't expect it to be."[26] Instead of envying the apparent success of the ungodly, young disciples' hearts break over their unsaved friends and even for the culture.

Grads know that being on mission will involve a lifelong battle against the evil one. Ephesians 6 reminds them that they must arm themselves against his "fiery darts" daily, expecting him and his demons to attack. They are realists.

Fully armed, disciple grads storm the gates of Hell. As Romans 12:1–2 puts it, they offer themselves as a living sacrifice to God. Their minds have been changed, transformed by this reality, so that God can show them His will, which is not merely good or even acceptable, but perfect (completely fulfilled).

Disciple grads war not against flesh and blood, as we are told in Ephesians 6. Instead, they are battling *"principalities and powers in high places."* Their fellow human beings are not the enemy; they are not tempted to confuse Satan with those hapless souls whom he *"has taken captive to do his will"* (2 Timothy 2:26). Their battle is for the souls of men, and they are engaged in the great rescue operation. Your disciple grads instinctively understand this and prepare themselves to rescue the perishing.

Grads are able to share their testimony and the Gospel effectively. They are always on mission and engaged in mission service however possible. They are deeply involved with the Kingdom's rescue operation, (Evangelism). God is all about lost souls. Jesus came to save people from the Devil's snare. Disciples follow Him into the fray.

Disciples do not engage in Great Commission work simply because they want to, but because they are compelled by the Holy Spirit. His love empowers them to share what they know (excuse me, Who they know) with those who are enshrouded in darkness.

Disciples are bold. As children, we sang, "This little light of mine, I'm gonna' let it shine." The Devil hates the Light, and disciples are painful to him because they are light in this world (Matthew 5:14). Just standing firmly with the light of Christ shining on disciples' faces causes Satan to flee (James 4:7).

In the end, disciple grads are overcomers. They have learned to consistently stand against and defeat the evil one. They have the scars to prove it. Disciple grads are dangerous to the Devil.

2. Graduates Competently Support God's Great Community (Encouraging).

Our second aspect of competency focuses on our disciples' work with others in the Church. Thank God, we do not march against the enemy alone. We value the Great Community where together we accomplish our goal to carry the light into dark places, reflecting God's glory into a fearful and hopeless world.

Disciple grads know that they are better together. We hope our disciples will have learned this very early. This will involve two important aspects. First, they embrace a sense of their dependency upon Christ and their need for others. They will not think more highly of themselves than they should. They humble themselves and carry one another's burdens (Galatians 6:2). They are sensitive to the individual needs of other believers and engage in prayer and caring ministry with others in various ways. They get under the load to help lift up the whole youth group.

Secondly, they have learned where they fit in God's army, His Church. They not only utilize practical skills to assist in the Body but also realize they have each been given gifts by the Spirit which enable them to work with others in the Body in amazing harmony. Your graduating disciples have explored, if not yet mastered, the use of their spiritual gifts. They have offered themselves and their giftedness to fellow soldiers as part of their common defense against the enemy. They do not all have the same gifts, just as every soldier is not outfitted for the same task. No disciple is ready for graduation until he has demonstrated a sense of interdependency with the Body. Disciples recognize that they need one another. They have learned to do their part for a mission that is far greater than themselves.

Summing Up

Disciple grads realize that in each of the three relationship areas we have covered, it is the Spirit who enables them to experience successful relationships. He alone produces the character of self-discipline, confidence in Scripture, and competencies to serve both in the world and in the Church. Ultimately, disciples rely upon the Holy Spirit for guidance in all their relationships. They walk in the Spirit because only He has the ability to enable their ultimate success in every relationship area:

- Equipping Relationship with the Savior: The Spirit provides power and guidance to fully embrace the Great Commandment.

- Evangelizing Relationships with lost souls: The Spirit produces the fruit of God's love in us to engage in the Great Commission.
- Encouraging Relationships with the saints: The Spirit prescribes gifts within the Great Community to enable us to serve effectively together in God's great enterprise.

As We Prepare to Close this Book and Open a New Chapter

We have acquainted ourselves as disciplers with a solid picture of what a spiritual young man or woman looks like. We will look for signs that they are ready for the next stage. No doubt, they will be chomping at the bit to lead others where they themselves are going. Once a person becomes consistent at the spiritual Accountability stage, it is unlikely that anything less than spiritual parenthood will be acceptable going forward. And that is the subject of the final book in this series. In that book, we will move on to examine spiritual Ability.

I truly have enjoyed partnering with you through these pages as you have considered how to disciple young people. I realize that there will be days when you will wonder if the hard work of discipleship is really worth it. Especially with young people. And especially if you live in a culture where discipling may be viewed as discriminatory, or asking too much, or unacceptably messy, or you name it.

Is there a reward for the diligent discipler? Trust me, there will be no greater rewards distributed in Heaven than for those who obeyed the Master's last command to go and make disciples of all nations. Paul wrote to the Thessalonians, *"For what is our hope, our joy, or the crown in which we will glory in the presence of our Lord Jesus when he comes? Is it not you? Indeed, you are our glory and joy*" (1 Thessalonians 2:19–20). Paul has not yet received his reward in full; it is still accruing to his account as his words and example continue to produce more disciples . . . and more rewards.

Start now. It will take you a while to get to the "explosion" part of dynamic youth ministry. The multiplication will begin—later. Don't miss it; don't delay it; don't ignore it. May the Lord greatly bless you for caring this much about the rising generation of believers!

I am praying for your journey.

EPILOGUE

Practical Next Steps for
Youth Leaders and Disciplers

Accountability is a vital and essential step in the right direction in youth ministry. We have described the marks of a grad-ready disciple, the hoped-for outcome of Accountability. But perhaps you are at the front end of all of this. You wonder where to begin. You may have just arrived to begin ministering with a new church. Or maybe you are already deep in the weeds at your current church and wonder how to squeeze discipleship into an already busy schedule. The first thing you will need to do is to pray for God's guidance. Take a deep breath. Remind yourself that you need only take one step at a time.

Ask the Father for guidance in these first steps. You want to plan for the long haul, not just the short-term. Multiplication takes time on the front end to gather speed, so you will want the right people onboard with you in this adventure. Oh, and yes, get ready for some disappointments. Both you and your disciple group members are only human. Expect a bit of stumbling here and there.

And on that note, whenever you place adults in the company of teenagers you will want to insist on background checks for those adults. Of course, this is not a foolproof guarantee against predatory behaviors, but it is certainly an obligatory and prudent first step. Beyond that, you will need to stay close enough to the adult volunteers to be more aware of their personal lives, their values, their behaviors. You may want to secure your pastor's input and oversight in the selection process. The pastor may well have insights that you would have missed. Two are better than one. Stay under pastoral authority. You get the picture.

Begin to look for disciple candidates. Perhaps you will want to begin with a small disciple group of young people that you lead personally before you ask others to join in. Better yet, you may choose to begin with a group of adult volunteers who will later each lead their own disciple groups. Parents or grandparents of teens, church elders, volunteer youth workers, schoolteachers, and college students could all be a rich resource for your first discipleship effort.

In any case, why not begin with a very small group, maybe only three or four disciples. Later, when your adults are ready to begin discipling teens, you can engage your adult volunteers to help lead in student discipleship. Let them team up to minister together. At one point, my wife and I joined another couple to disciple two groups in our house at the same time. The guys met in the kitchen (where the snacks were) while the girls met with the two ladies in the living room. We were together initially for a few things (food, ha). Then we met separately, guys with guys and girls with girls.

In your own situation, perhaps two adult disciplers could team up with a few young people for discipleship. This team approach also allows your adults whom you have discipled to then disciple teens together and experiment and apply what they have learned in a team effort.

Accountability is Not the End Goal

Remember: Accountability is a means to a greater goal. After all, Accountability implies that your disciples are, well, being held accountable. That means someone has to do the job of holding them accountable. See what I mean? We don't want the job of overseeing our young disciples forever. That is definitely *not* what we hope for as the final product of our discipleship with young people. We hope for more.

More? Even more than self-discipline? Absolutely.

Of course, we all hope for that time to arrive when our own children have become fully responsible for their personal lives. We want to know that they are able to make wise decisions and to choose godly living. (Helicopter moms may possibly be the exception?) But then what? There is another level, and it is really exciting. We call it the Ability stage.

Any parent will tell you that they hope to someday have grandchildren! I have reached that enviable stage in life; I am now "Pop" to my amazing grandkids, and yes, I have pictures. They are special beyond belief and would likely put others' grandkids to shame. Just saying.

The goal of discipleship is that your protégés reproduce spiritual children. That they bring the Holy Spirit's gift of new life to those who are otherwise the walking dead. We want the discipleship process to energize their own quest to disciple others, hopefully those whom they have personally led to faith in Jesus.

I hope you have been challenged to begin the journey with several young people into the adventure of discipleship. But once that process is complete, they will have a lifetime of service ahead of them. They will need mentors along the way, perhaps different ones at different stages along the journey.

I have found that once the discipleship relationship has concluded, my young disciples continue to contact me for a variety of things. At that point, we have entered into a different type of relationship together, the realm of mentoring. And it is very rewarding.

One young man, Cam Boothe, was an intern at the Global Institute. Watching him grow in Christ was a special blessing. Now, he is actively and effectively engaging in discipleship that produces disciplers, not just disciples. I still maintain an active friendship with Cam. I have the joy of visiting him or talking with him by phone quite often.

Cam began to disciple others while he was in his early twenties. They now call him Grandpa because so many generations of disciples have already followed after his initial disciple group. That first group of guys went and found others to disciple. Now, that is what we are talking about! May his tribe increase.

Multiplication! Isn't that the real goal? My personal experience has been that spiritual multiplication occurs much more rapidly than I had expected. After all, it potentially will take perhaps one or two years to prepare a disciple to go out and make disciples on his own. Sooner than you think, you may find yourself surrounded by several generations of disciples! What a prospect! What a grand reunion awaits when we all get together in Heaven, God's house, His forever family gathered around the throne of Jesus!

My fervent hope is that our young disciples engage in discipling others just as they were themselves discipled. That is the huge endgame for discipleship.

Just like Jesus, we want our young disciples to go into their world to make disciples. We desire to make disciples who become disciple makers. Mentoring will be the subject of the final book in this series, a study of what it means to help spiritually effective young warriors take the next step into the ministry of disciple-making.

Nothing about Jesus' last Great Commission has changed. Except for one thing: we have less time to fulfill it. Everything is on the line. May God grant you the will to continue through thick and thin. May it be your special privilege to see several generations of disciples rise to continue the work until Jesus returns!

ADDITIONAL
RESOURCES

REFLECTION GUIDE

CHAPTER 1—WHAT IF YOUR YOUTH MINISTRY COULD SOAR?

(pages 23-39)

1. The spiritual stages of maturity listed in 1 John 2:12–14 include children (Availability), young men (Accountability), and fathers (Ability). Another stage was listed which consists of students who have not yet been reborn, spiritual Apathy. After a careful and prayerful review of these spiritual levels, how would you characterize the general personality of your group? Where are the majority currently parked? Make a list of your students and prayerfully place them in the four stages as best as you are able.

2. As you consider where your youth group is parked, do you desire to move them toward a multi-stage family of faith? Do you embrace the need for discipleship? Why or why not?

3. There were several positive and negative indicators that a few of the students in your group may be seeking discipleship. Do you see any of these indicators among your teens?

4. If you do not see indications of readiness for discipleship, what are some ways you and your leadership team could "salt the oats" to motivate them?

5. Make a list of potential disciple candidates (see Appendix).

CHAPTER 2—IS DISCIPLESHIP REALLY THE SECRET?

(pages 40-49)

1. Jesus gave us one Great Commission, to go and make disciples. Is your church engaging or accomplishing this? How would you rate your church's prioritizing of discipleship? Do your youth members and parents participate actively in this endeavor? Why or why not?

2. Growth is inherently part of life and health. Are your teens growing spiritually, or are they stagnant, dependent, or even listless about spiritual things?

3. Discipleship is not the end goal. Your task is to prepare your students for Evangelizing and Encouraging other people. It's not about us! Is discipleship a secret to your youth group members? Why or why not?

4. Which of the four reasons why discipleship should not be a secret seems to be the best kept secret to your group?

4. Write a brief description of what you would say to teens about becoming discipled.

CHAPTER 3—DEFINING DYNAMIC DISCIPLESHIP

(pages 50-64)

1. Discipleship is not a second Sunday school, small group, academic class, etc. Has this chapter helped you to distinguish discipleship from these activities? Do you

agree that we must NOT call any small group meeting discipleship? Discipleship should be a step-up!

2. Discipleship must have a motivating prize to attract participation. In 2 Timothy 2:2, the author offered two motivations for engaging in discipleship. The first was the privilege to hang out with and learn from an older, wiser believer. The second was the prospect of someday leading others as a discipler. Do you see these as sufficient motivators for your teens? Why or why not?

3. Some of the qualities of a discipler were outlined in this chapter. What would you add or delete or change on the list? Do you qualify? It was stated that there must be something magnetic about a discipler's walk with Jesus. Are you willing to make necessary adjustments to grow? What should you be doing to improve your spiritual magnetism?

CHAPTER 4—WHY DISCIPLESHIP ISN'T DONE

(pages 67-80)

1. Discipleship is costly for disciples. Sometimes churches want to make everything available to everyone at no cost. Do you agree with this concept, and that discipleship should be open to all regardless of their commitment level? Why or why not?

2. The discipler also pays a price in terms of being scrutinized, the loss of privacy and personal time, and being held to a higher standard. Which of these is the greatest concern to you? Why?

3. How do you resonate with the idea of having only one disciple group meeting per week, but requiring more

daily effort and involvement from your disciples both individually and in the ongoing youth program?

4. How you spend time is of the utmost importance. What steps will you need to take to allow time for discipleship?

5. As you prepare to disciple teens, what weekly meeting time do you think would work best for you and for them?

CHAPTER 5—MAKING DISCIPLESHIP DOABLE

(pages 81-90)

1. Your Availability stage group members should get incentives to move toward Accountability. Some suggestions were given. List other ways you could incentivize your teens to step up in their spiritual growth.

2. Students must want discipleship; it cannot be forced. The Book says we should "find and feed the hungry." If you have already created a list of potential disciples, begin to pray for their spiritual hunger.

3. It is recommended that you thoroughly interview every potential young disciple. What are some important questions you would want to ask students individually?

4. One challenge in discipleship is the false claim of playing favorites. What precautions will you take to prevent legitimate accusations of favoritism?

5. Parents may express concerns about time commitments. But worse, they may be concerned about their students becoming too religious or too spiritual. What could you do to properly educate parents in your church about the integration of faith with other pursuits?

CHAPTER 6—DISCIPLESHIP RELATIONSHIPS

(pages 91-104)

1. The first essential relationship is Equipping students in their relationship with God through Scripture and prayer. Why are these two resources so important in our walk with Jesus? The author says this relationship comes before all others. Do you agree? Why or why not?

2. Evangelizing relationships are with people who dwell in darkness. Our works of service are designed to demonstrate the love of Christ to a waiting world. But is serving them enough? Do you agree that we must lead disciples to speak of Jesus to them individually and verbally?

3. The final relationship is with the Body of believers to edify or Encourage (instill courage in) them. We should guide disciples to work together as one unit to carry out our mission in the world. Do you agree?

4. The number of disciples must be limited because these relationships will take time and effort to develop. Have you thought through the amount of time you will need to commit to discipleship? What about extra casual or spontaneous times (beyond a regular meeting) when you can build relationships with your disciples?

5. The author suggests that it will take time to finish the job of discipleship. What length of weeks or even months do you think plan to allot in order to accomplish the task?

6. The author recommends a smaller number of teens to disciple, at least at first. How many do you think you can manage in a disciple team?

7. The best place for discipling students is wherever you live, work, and play. How do you feel about regularly having

students in your home or with you in your daily activities?
Is your family in agreement?

CHAPTER 7—YOUR DISCIPLES' PERSONAL GUIDE

(pages 107-119)

1. The key to following Christ is to learn to listen to His voice inside us. How well do you as a discipler listen daily to the Spirit? What do you need to do to follow the Spirit more closely?

2. The discipline of listening to the Spirit is especially difficult in today's world. In what ways do you observe this reality among young people?

3. How will you begin to guide your disciples to be better listeners? Are there specific assignments you can give to them, like setting aside media devices or online interaction for a season? What else?

CHAPTER 8—DESIRING SELF-DISCIPLINE

(pages 120-136)

1. Discipleship must not be limited to just one dimension. It consists of character development, Scriptural competency, and servant leader competencies. These are mentioned in John's description of "spiritual young men" in 1 John 2:12-14. We must start with character, developing self-disciplines in our young disciples. How do you feel about this task and how will you approach it?

2. Of the four self-disciplines that are covered, which one do you feel most qualified to help your young disciples? Least qualified?

3. Which of the four areas of self-discipline do you believe will be the most difficult one for your disciples to master? Why?

CHAPTER 9—DISCIPLING LIKE JESUS

(pages 137-154)

1. Certainly, there is a place for formal learning in discipleship. But the author believes that sometimes this takes too great a percentage of the discipling process. What do you think?

2. Teachable moments can only come when we are walking together with our disciples in the midst of daily life. How will you up your game in this area? List ways you could use normal activities to teach your disciples about life in Christ (not just at a meeting with them)?

3. What are some field trips that you could take with your disciples to give them opportunities to see other people in need and to be inspired by others who have moved forward in their walk with Jesus?

4. Examinations are good for disciples. What are some areas in which your disciples will likely need to be tested? Where could you take them or what tasks could you give them that would test their capacities or reveal weak areas?

5. The author listed several topics for your disciples. What do you think was left out? What should be added to the list of topics? Make your own list of basic topics your disciples need to cover. Begin a list of possible teaching resources for these topics.

CHAPTER 10—WHO, ME? A SOLDIER?

(pages 157-172)

1. The book suggests that we have greatly downplayed the reality of sin and Hell in the modern Church. Do you agree with this assessment?

2. The enemy is Satan, not people whom he has taken captive to do his will (2 Timothy 2:26). Do you agree that believers sometimes get this mixed up? Do your teenagers know the difference? How will you help them to distinguish?

3. The soldiers are the teens themselves. They have a mission to fulfill—to restore God's creation to reflect His Character. They do this by carrying His compassion to others. How do you feel about love (the fruit of the Spirit) being our weapon to rescue the lost?

4. We must lead disciples to engage in combat in the great rescue operation. Do you believe this is essential to discipleship? Why or why not?

5. How will you help your disciples identify specific mission fields that fit their life interests, schedules, and personalities?

CHAPTER 11—THE WORLD'S MOST STRATEGIC BATTLEFIELD

(pages 173-186)

1. The odds do not seem to favor godly teens in our culture who face worldly influences, technology, medical and drug challenges, and more. Can you think of specific challenges your teenagers face?

2. The great battleground is our teenage culture, especially the schools. The author suggests personal mission ministry as a step beyond group outreach activities for young disciples. Do you agree?

3. What are some ways your student disciples can minister to their unchurched friends and acquaintances away from church?

4. How do parents factor into your efforts to engage your disciples to reach out to lost people? How will you respond to their concerns?

5. How do you believe your disciples will respond initially to the idea of being held responsible for personal mission ministry? How can you help them get over the hump?

CHAPTER 12—DISCIPLES FINDING THEIR PLACE

(pages 189-200)

1. The author says we all need the fellowship of the Body of believers. Do you agree with this? How would you plan to involve your disciples in Body life?

2. To Encourage means to "instill courage." How does this inform how you will guide your disciples in this third essential relationship?

3. The author described disciples as the ones who get underneath the youth group to lift up its members. Do you agree or disagree with this perspective?

3. Lowly tasks are useful to instill humility in disciples. Do you agree that small tasks for your disciples will be helpful? What tasks could you design to help them move toward a more servant-like spirit?

CHAPTER 13—SERVANT TEAMS: MOVING INTO SPIRITUAL GIFTS

(pages 201-215)

1. According to the author, the Church seems to have turned over much of its work to professional staff. The rest of the congregation merely sits and watches. Do you agree with this assessment? Why or why not?

2. Several models of youth ministry were covered. Which model is most like your church's model for conducting its ministry with youth? Does this need to be adjusted or improved in your congregation? If so, how?

3. The key to your disciples finding their place is to discover their giftedness in the Body of Christ. The author says we cannot find true fulfillment apart from our spiritual gifts. How do you respond to that?

4. When disciples exercise their gifts, they find fulfillment by gaining competence. Do you believe that finding their spiritual gifts will play an important role in our disciples' sense of fulfillment in the Body. . . and in life?

5. Spiritual gifts ultimately instill courage for the rescue mission that lies outside the church doors. Do your disciples need courage to face life in modern culture? How will you expose them to opportunities with each other to learn their gifts?

CHAPTER 14—LAUNCH DATE

(pages 219-234)

1. The author outlines three primary ways to discern your disciples' readiness for the next stage, Ability: Character, Content, and Competencies. In which of these are your disciples most advanced? What do they lack?

2. As you prepare your disciples for "graduation" to the next level, leadership in disciple-making, how can you help them participate in determining their individual "readiness quotient?"

3. If you are a youth leader in a church, how will you begin engaging in discipleship with both adults and young people in your situation?

NOTES

Chapter 2—Is Discipleship Really The Secret?

1. Zuck, Roy B, and Benson, Warren S., *Youth Education in the Church*. Chicago: Moody Press, 1978), 57.
2. Dean, Kenda Creasy, *Almost Christian: What the Faith of our Teenagers Is Telling the American Church* (Oxford: Oxford University Press, 2010). Cop.

Chapter 3—Defining Dynamic Discipleship

3. Gravitt, Justin G., Discipleship org. 2022. "What Is Disciple Making, Precisely?" Discipleship.org. April 19, 2022. https: //discipleship.org/blog/what-is-disciple-making-precisely/.
4. Whitney, Donald S. *Spiritual Disciplines for the Christian Life*. Colorado Springs, CO: NavPress, 1991). 1.
5. Nappa, Mike. 1999. *What I Wish My Youth Leader Knew about Youth Ministry: A National Survey.* Cincinnati, Ohio: Standard Pub., 187.
6. Crabb, Lawrence J. 1988. *Understanding People*. Marshall Pickering, 110.

Chapter 4—Why Discipleship Isn't Done

7. Trueman, Carl R. 2022. *Strange New World: How Thinkers and Activists Redefined Identity and Sparked the Sexual Revolution.* Wheaton, Illinois: Crossway, 23.

8. Breen, Mike. 2017. *Building a Discipling Culture: How to Release a Missional Movement by Discipling People like Jesus Did.* Greenville, South Carolina: 3Dm Publishing.

Chapter 7—Your Disciples' Personal Guide

9. Harrington, Bobby, and Josh. 2017. *The Disciple Maker's Handbook: 7 Elements of a Discipleship Lifestyle.* Grand Rapids, Michigan: Zondervan.

10. Moody, Dwight L. 1884. *The Way to God and How to Find it.* Chicago, Illinois: F.H. Revell Publishers, 46.

Chapter 8—Desiring Self-Discipline

11. Wilder, Jim and Marcus Warner. 2016. *Rare Leadership: 4 Uncommon Habits for Increasing Trust, Joy, and Engagement in the People You Lead* Chicago: Moody Press, 115.

12. Elmore, Tim. 2023. "How Parents Steal from Their Kids." Growing Leaders. February 28, 2023. https: // growingleaders.com/how-parents-steal-from-their-kids/.

Chapter 9—Discipling Like Jesus

13. Rahn, Dave, and Ebonie Davis. 2020. *Disrupting Teens with Joy: Helping Youth Discover Jesus-Focused, Gritty Faith.* San Diego: The Youth Cartel, 112.

Chapter 10 –Who, Me? A Soldier?

14. Wiele, Gary Vander. 2023. "Helping Students Connect the Gospel with Their Brokenness." YM360. March 20, 2023. https: //youthministry360. com/blogs/all/helping-students-connect-the-gospel-with-their-brokenness.

15. "A Quote by C.S. Lewis." n.d. www.goodreads.com. Accessed April 19, 2023. https: //www.goodreads.com/quotes/755193-there-is-no-neutral-ground-in-the-universe-every-square.

16. Shaeffer, Francis. 1984. The Great Evangelical Disaster. Westchester, Illinois: Crossway Books, 31.

17. Adams, Ken, Discipleship org. 2022. "The Most Important Metric." Discipleship.org. December 21, 2022. https: //discipleship.org/blog/the-most-important-metric/.

Chapter 11—The World's Most Strategic Battlefield

18. Cooper, Brett. 2021. "CDC Reports 51% Increase in Suicide Attempts among Teenage Girls | Brett Cooper." Fee.org. June 25, 2021. https: //fee.org/articles/cdc-reports-51-increase-in-suicide-attempts-among-teenage-girls/.

19. News, A.B.C. n.d. "Opioid Overdose Deaths among Teens Have Skyrocketed due to Fentanyl." ABC News. https: //abcnews.go.com/Health/opioid-overdose-deaths-teens-skyrocketed-due-fentanyl/story? id=84035862.

20. Richardson, Bradford. March 27, 2018. "Link between Mass Shooters, Absent Fathers Ignored by Anti-Gun Activists." The Washington Times. https://www.washingtontimes.com/news/2018/mar/27/mass-shooters-absent-fathers-link-ignored-anti-gun/.

Chapter 12—Disciples Finding Their Place

21. Crabb, Lawrence J. 1988. *Understanding People*. Marshall Pickering, 110.

22. Kitchings, Hal. March 24, 2023. "3 Reasons to Get back to Church!" www.medishare.com. Accessed April 19, 2023.
    https: //www.medishare.com/
    blog/3-reasons-to-get-back-to-church.

23. Cathy, Truett. https://www.chick-fil-a.com/stories/ inside-chick-fil-a/2015/11/09/inspire-more-people. Truett Cathy's unexpected approach to business and life | Chick-fil-A.

24. Crabb, Lawrence J. 1988. *Understanding People*. Marshall Pickering, 114.

Chapter 13—Servant Teams: Moving Into Spiritual Gifts

25. Wilterdink, Chris. 2016. *Everyday Disciples: Covenant Discipleship with Youth*. Upper Room Books.

Chapter 14—Launch Date

26. Lucado, Max. 2012. "Heaven: God's Highest Hope." Max Lucado. March 22, 2012.
    https: //maxlucado.com/heaven-gods highest-hope/.

DISCIPLE POSSIBILITIES

On this page write names of students whom you believe to be possible candidates for your disciple group. Begin to pray over these names.

STUDENT'S NAME	AGE/ GRADE	PRAYER NOTES

DISCIPLESHIP INTERVIEW QUESTIONS

Eligibility Questions

1. What is your current age/grade in school?
2. What other routine activities do you take part in beyond church activities?
3. Would anything, either ongoing activities or single events, prevent you from participating fully in the discipleship program?
4. After reading the Disciple Covenant, is there anything in it that gives you concern or makes you feel hesitant or unwilling to participate in discipleship?

Interest Questions

1. Why would you want to be part of discipleship?
2. In what areas or in what ways would you most like to grow during our discipleship time together?
3. What, if anything, concerns you about being part of an Accountability level group?
4. Do you see and welcome the value of passing on to others what you are learning about following Jesus?

DISCIPLESHIP COVENANT

As a part of this disciple team, I agree to honor these commitments, not only for my sake and for my fellow disciple teammates, but for the Kingdom.

1. I covenant before the Lord to become truly available to Him in all areas of my life by entering into a time of growth and maturing that will bring honor to Him.
2. I covenant to meet faithfully with my disciple teammates for at least one group time per week as described by my discipler. I will be present and ready to participate faithfully.
3. I will fulfill all my obligations with a spirit of cooperation and honesty, whether it is reading, memorizing, participating in mission, witness, or ministry, completing all assignments in a timely way and be ready to participate fully each week with my team.
4. I covenant to honor confidentiality with my disciple teammates and discipler, and to be transparent and honest with them in my personal spiritual growth and struggles.
5. I will pray regularly for my discipler and my disciple teammates.

6. I will seek not only to become a faithful disciple but will also begin now praying for God to point me to others that I may disciple at the appropriate time.

Disciple

Date: _____ / _____ / _____

Discipler

Date: _____ / _____ / _____

BOOKS BY THE AUTHOR . . .

This book is part of a series that has but one purpose, to help your youth ministry become part of something greater, God's glory. As we often say here at the Global Institute for Youth Leadership, it is better to learn from mistakes . . . other people's mistakes, that is! And that is why these books were written, based upon much study of the Word and too many mistakes! Our purpose is to help fellow youth leaders jump-start youth ministry that lasts and contributes effectively to His Kingdom!

- *Growing Up: Youth Ministry Coming of Age* (A case for youth ministry in God's great plan to reach the world).
- *The Master's Call to Global Youth Ministry* (Considering your place in God's mission to spread the Good News to every teen).
- *Youth Ministry By The Book* (Exploring biblical principles for youth ministry);
- *ReGroup! Building Youth Ministry from the Bible UP* (A simple place to begin a youth ministry that helps build strategically for future growth).
- *Dynamic Discipleship: The "Secret" to Explosive Youth Ministry* (Moving your youth group toward robust growth at the middle Accountability growth stage).

Made in the USA
Middletown, DE
30 August 2024

60001175R00146